D0901701

RADHA
Diary of a Woman's Search

Other Books by the Author

Kundalini Yoga for the West
Hatha Yoga: The Hidden Language
The Hatha Yoga Workbook
Mantras: Words of Power
Seeds of Light
The Divine Light Invocation

Timeless Books
Box 50905
Palo Alto, CA 94303-0673
(415) 321-8311 or (604) 227-9224

Write or call for our free catalog of books,
audio tapes, video tapes and more.

RADHA
Diary of a Woman's Search

Swami Sivananda Radha
(Sylvia Hellman)

Timeless Books

1990

P.O. Box 50905 Palo Alto, CA 94303-9224

Photographs by Swami Saradananda, Rishikesh, India
Book design by Richard A. Reeves
Cover design by Cynthia Poole and Linda Anne Seville

Printed in the United States of America
Previous printings: 1981, 1983

Third printing 1990

Library of Congress Cataloging in Publication Data
Sivananda Radha, Swami, 1911-
    Radha, diary of a woman's search / Swami Sivananda Radha
(Sylvia Hellman).
        p.   cm.
   ISBN 0-931454-19-0 : $13.95
    1. Sivananda Radha, Swami, 1911-   --Diaries. 2. Yogis--
Diaries. 3. Sivananda, Swami. 4. Yoga. I. Title.
   BL 1175.S52A37   1990
   294.5' 092--dc20
   [B]   90-32272

Published by

Timeless Books

Box 50905
Palo Alto, CA 94303-0673

Dedicated . . .

To all the Gurus who have prepared the Path,
Especially the Most Precious One
Swami Sivananda Saraswati of Rishikesh, India.

Table of Contents

Illustrations

Foreword

Discipleship is an adventure. Discipleship of an enlightened sage is a great adventure. Discipleship of an enlightened sage like Gurudev Swami Sivananda is an extraordinary adventure.

How was Swami Sivananda extraordinary? Enlightenment blended in him with limitless compassion and intense dynamism, with the result that he was the confluence of apparent contradictions. In him they became complementary and fascinating. His actions were as unpredictable as his wisdom was unfathomable. And this kept his disciples on their toes all the time, ever alert, never taking the Master and his teachings for granted and never falling into the rut of a patterned behavior.

Moreover, Swami Sivananda's dazzling personality had so many facets that to serve him was a rare education and real test. He was a medical man turned mystic, an intellectual with an intuitive understanding, an astute administrator who lived absolute renunciation, a scientist, and a sage. His love and compassion flooded the disciple's heart, eroding and eradicating the ego.

Many of Swami Sivananda's close disciples spent years at the feet of the Master. They and he had all the time in the world, as it were, for the chiseling and the sculpturing needed to liberate the Divine within. But Swami Radha had to take the training in an intense and compressed way, in a few months. It was not easy for either the guru or the disciple.

It would be no exaggeration to say that, during the period of Swami Radha's first visit to the Sivananda Ashram, she was constantly in the Master's mind. He was her mother, anxious to ensure her well-being. He was her host who provided her with comfort, as much as an austere ashram could afford. He was her teacher who ensured that she had the right instruction in all branches of yoga, including music. He was her guru intent on turning her gaze towards the light and on ensuring that it stayed unwaveringly illumined.

For her part, Swami Radha had *quickly* to shed her own "back-ground" and her conditioning, to learn a totally new way of looking at life, at human relationships and at salvation or perfection.

The innate wisdom in Swami Radha guided her to the only way all this could be accomplished *quickly*: total dedication to the guru and implicit obedience. On one or two occasions, when her own mind "questioned" the guru's practice or precept, her wisdom immediately revealed the unwisdom of such an attitude. She rejected it and it was washed away with a few tears.

Out of these tears rose Radha. Swami Sivananda must have seen her resurrection and hence christened her "Radha." Of all the devotees of Lord Krishna in his own time, Radha was the foremost; she had no thought for herself and lived in and for Lord Krishna in utter self-surrender and dedication. Even so, Swami Radha had totally surrendered to Gurudev Swami Sivananda.

Very soon after that, Swami Radha experienced the miracle of such surrender. Not only the learned and saintly disciples of Swami Sivananda, but also other holy men and women of India received and instructed her: nay, Swami Sivananda himself appeared in all those forms to carry on and complete the spiritual education of his disciple. Swami Radha saw her guru in Swami Purushatthamananda, in Ma Anandamoyi, in Swami Ramdas and in the Tibetan Yogi. They inspired her and instructed her. But it was Swami Sivananda who worked through them.

The Master often described the best disciple as one who preserves, promotes and propagates the guru's teaching. When Swami Sivananda asked Swami Radha to start an ashram in Canada, she immediately answered "Yes." With single-minded devotion and dedication she has achieved it. She even now remembers every single word that the Master said to her, and with an extraordinary genius she has woven the Master's teaching into highly practical and scientific techniques which she teaches during her own workshops.

In the words of the Kathopanishad, "The Master was unique and wonderful; the disciple is unique and wonderful, too."

Swami Venkatesananda
Mauritius, Indian Ocean

Preface

Hardly anyone can go through life without encountering, more than once, the feeling that something basic is missing and that nothing really makes sense. So many things seem to need doing, all very important and seemingly endless. If we are lucky, from time to time we get a glimpse of an elusive, underlying meaning of life, different for each of us, and yet something that glimmers through for a moment, dispelling the unnerving feeling that we are leading an empty, meaningless existence. As long as ego-centered concerns, hopes and fears, block our view, this kind of insight is rare. We need to get a distance from ourselves, to go at least mentally on a pilgrimage.

This is as far as probably any reader will agree, but then some questions are bound to crop up to some persons—why would anyone really want to go to India, live in an Indian monastery for a while, and, above all, why would a woman wish to do all this? We all know how socially restricted the life of most women in India is. While young, they can never go anywhere if not accompanied by persons in charge of them; they have hardly any say in matters that concern them, as for instance in the selection of the husband whom they have to marry; and once they are married, they are completely the responsibility of their in-laws, must try to serve them to the best of their ability and hope to produce one or more sons desired for the continuation of the family. What can a country where such old-fashioned ideas concerning women prevail, teach a highly educated Western woman; what can she learn there? All this is superficially true, but on closer inspection the restrictions for women in India are not nearly as all-pervading as they appeared at first; moreover they are largely the result of her parents' and her family's concern for her security and welfare. She often nowadays receives adequate education, if she comes from a good family, and if, on that basis, she is able to secure employment, she can refuse an arranged marriage and live her own life, obtaining often a highly respected position.

But far more important than this is the fact that, from a spiritual viewpoint, woman in India was never considered as inferior to man or secondrate. For most thinkers in the West woman has for centuries been considered an intruder who has no right to enter man's world of thought. Even to this day few thinkers would go as far as V. Soloview in *Le sense de l'amour*, when he speaks of "The intrinsic understanding that woman is as essential to man as he is to her." For India, on the other hand, this has been a basic idea, expressed concisely in the Brhadaranyaka Upanisad: "In the beginning, this (universe) was but the *viraj* (shining) of a human form. He reflected and found nothing but himself. . . .He was not at all happy. Therefore people (still) are not happy when alone. He desired a mate. He became as big as man and wife embracing each other. He parted this very body in two. From that came husband and wife. Therefore, said Yajnavalkya, this (body) is one-half of oneself, like of the two halves of a split pea. Therefore this space is indeed filled by the wife. He was united with her. From that men were born." What is meant by this somewhat cryptic remark is brought out more clearly by Madhu Khanna in his explanation to Saiva Purana: "Just as moonbeams cannot be separated from the moon nor the rays from the sun, so Sakti cannot be distinguished from Siva. So close is their interrelation that there can be no Siva without Sakti and no Sakti without Siva. This cosmic biunity is parallelled by 'psychic biunity' in the human male and female, and suggests that there is necessarily feminine in every man and masculine in every woman as partial illumination of a whole." This thought found expression in Indian art and literature. Siva, the god, has been many times depicted as Ardhanarisvara, that is half man, half woman, both Siva and Parvati (Sakti) at the same time; Kalidasa, the greatest Indian poet, took up this idea when explaining why Siva can adopt both the posture of *lasya*—the sensuously seductive mode—and *tandava*—the violent or terrifying mode.

Even more strongly have the underlying ideas of man and woman, originating from a basic unity and remaining in harmony with it, found their expression in the myth of Radha and Krishna which has given continued inspiration to literature and art in India. It is expressed, for example, in the Rajput and Kangra paintings, justifiably famous for their beauty and tenderness of mood. Here again, Radha is as important as Krishna and also as the environment, all forming an indissoluble unity that would be meaningless if one of the aspects were missing. As P. Banerjee states in *The Life of Krishna in Indian Art*, "The chief object of the. . .sect is. . .Krishna, the supreme god, who appeared in Vrindavana in the form of Radha and Krishna. His soul is Radha, mind is Krishna, the body is vrindavana and the sense organs are the Sakhis (female friends or companions)."

A sustaining trend in Indian thought has always been the awareness that life becomes meaningless if one part of the personality is given undue preference at the expense of other, that only an understanding of the complete personality can help a person to achieve anything, and that no essential part needs to be or should be excluded or put in a very subordinate position. Some of the outstanding philosophers such as Sankara and Bhartrhari, have used poetry to express in beautiful, emotionally moving language some of their loftiest thoughts. And although relatively few women in India have become renouned philosophers or visionaries, those who did, like Gargi and Mirabai, have earned the highest recognition and respect for their outstanding achievements.

Important as these thoughts on men and women have always been in India, a foreigner residing there only a limited time would hardly become aware of them. Indeed, if he somehow did get a glimpse of them, he would find this glimpse utterly unintelligible and contrary to all that he had learned before. For Swami Radha the situation was entirely different; she encountered the richness of India's view of life at every step and, guided by her strong intuitive understanding as well as by her guru and the other teachers whom she met there, she found nothing strange in these ideas and could appreciate fully all that was implied. Besides, this was only a small part of the incredible amount of factual instruction for which she had come to India, knowing that correct, authentic information would be needed later if she was to help others gain access to the meaningful way of life she had found for herself.

The present book gives a clear account of Swami Radha's stay in the Ashram in Rishikesh—a deeply satisfying time when suddenly things fell into place, doubts were dispelled, and the task of helping others was entrusted to her that has proved increasingly more important. Taking the cue from Swami Radha, the reader is left with no doubts about the true meaning of the complete renunciation of ego-centred preferences and concerns that is needed on a spiritual path. On the other hand, the reader will not be bothered with mystifying language or concepts; the path that is outlined here involves, as her Guru Swami Sivananda explained, a methodically developed procedure which, if correctly followed, is bound to have positive results. The diary form, too, was suggested by her guru. Impressions lose their freshness if not related immediately. Moreover, a diary gives the person a chance to take stock of what he is learning and of his own reactions.

Apart from the immediate instructions by her Guru and other teachers she met, Swami Radha's stay in India presented a challenge in itself. Living conditions are often quite austere; a soft bed to sleep on became suddenly an unobtainable luxury, pleasantly satisfying food a problem (this would apply no less to the people living in India all the time who have to solve it by either eating only what they cook for themselves or what a very trusted servant prepares for them). India's acceptance of life in many shapes and forms accounts for the tolerance not only of the mischievous and thievish monkeys, the cows that certainly have the right of way on all highways, shopping areas and public places, but also of a rich insect life including huge scorpions and spiders. Startling as encounters with unusual animals may often be, they add spice to life and help to put our views into perspective, showing us that we human beings are not the only ones that have a right to live. It is the vivid descriptions of encounters with all sorts of creatures that provides the lighter side of the book.

First and foremost, however, the book is centered around Swami Sivananda, a highly respected spiritual teacher in India, his sympathetic understanding and warmhearted personality, and his way of training disciples and followers. Swami Radha's unassuming way of dealing with the topic of her pilgrimage, her clarity of presentation, and her thorough sincerity may well be considered as a major contribution.

Ilse Guenther, Ph. D.
Saskatoon, Saskatchewan

Introduction

This account of Swami Sivananda Radha's pilgrimage to India is of special value for Westerners seriously interested in yoga and other spiritual disciplines. Born and raised in Europe, Swami Radha studied with and received initiation from Swami Sivananda, who is regarded as one of India's greatest yogis. Since returning to the West, she has lived the life of a renunciant and spiritual teacher for the past 25 years. She is able to explain and to translate the yogic tradition as only a Westerner who has fully immersed herself in that tradition can.

Swami Radha was born in Berlin, in 1911, into a liberal, wealthy German family. In 1939, she was the first woman admitted to the Berlin School of Advertising. Radha's career was cut short by her opposition to the Nazis. After the war, she emigrated to Canada, where she first came in contact with her guru, Swami Sivananda, in a vision that appeared to her in meditation.

Radha began to correspond with Swami Sivananda. His letters affected her powerfully, and she decided to leave everything behind and follow his advice to "come home" to his ashram in Rishikesh, in the Himalayan foothills. Her stay in India was a time of intense spiritual practice and discipline, in a dedicated community that included advanced students as well as real masters of various spiritual disciplines.

On her return to Canada, Radha continued her spiritual practices; she also followed her guru's instructions to spread the teachings of yoga in the West. Swami Radha has developed a great many truly innovative approaches for psychological and spiritual development, adapted from her training in India. One of these is the Life Seal, a powerful form of self-exploration through the development of one's own mandala, using symbols drawn to represent different levels of personality. Other courses and workshops include the Straight Walk, adapted from an ancient Buddhist practice designed to clarify thinking and perception, an Ideals Workshop, and training in dream understanding.

Swami Radha has also founded a flourishing spiritual community in Canada. Yasodhara Ashram, located on the shores of Kootenay Bay in British Columbia, is, in many ways an amalgam of the best of East and West. The residents have built virtually everything by hand, including exquisitely constructed two-story residence and guest buildings. Courses and weekend workshops developed by Swami Radha are given regularly, along with courses offered by distinguished guest instructors, such as Dr. Herbert Guenther. A three-month yoga teachers' training course and a six-week yoga growth intensive stress serious self-examination and clarity of thinking. I have personally learned a great deal from Swami Radha's grounded approach to spiritual growth, and her insistence that self-realization be based on real self-understanding, and not merely a series of spiritual "highs."

My first contact with Swami Radha occurred through her extraordinarily beautiful and powerful recording, *Mantras, Songs of Yoga,* which I have listened to for many years. I first met her in person in 1974, at a conference on consciousness and related topics. She was dressed in Western clothing, with none of the obvious symbols of her monastic status. Her talks were of great depth and value, yet devoid of ostentation. When she discussed the chakras, Swami Radha spoke with a kind of insight and clarity that seemed to come from actually experiencing each chakra from the inside. I began to see more and more clearly the wisdom and spiritual stature hidden behind her quiet and gracious nature.

This book provides an inspiring account of Swami Radha's initiation into the Divine Light Invocation as well as a wide variety of other spiritual experiences. It is taken from the diary she kept faithfully throughout her stay in India. From her initial discomfort and discontent, we gradually witness an inner transformation that brings her to view her surroundings in a very different light. The powerful spiritual atmosphere of Sivananda's ashram becomes more and more evident as Swami Radha herself changes.

Swami Sivananda himself is glimpsed in many roles—as a busy administrator, as playful and sometimes exasperatingly arbitrary or indirect, and also as a great spiritual master and a deeply compassionate guru, whose love flowed continuously to his disciples and whose discipline was all the more powerful for its subtlety.

The reader can follow Swami Radha's inner unfolding as she copes with numerous doubts and difficulties. Her struggles to understand her guru range from the comical to heartrending. Throughout, we can see the interplay between the mundane, often frustrating outer realities, and the deeper spiritual reality underlying all the activities of the ashram. In so honestly recounting her own journey, Swami Radha reminds us all of the truth and power of that deeper reality and of the ways we can remain in tune with it in our own lives.

Robert Frager Ph. D.
Founder and Director,
California Institute of Transpersonal Psychology

RADHA
Diary of a Woman's Search

31 August, 1955 to 1 March 1956

31 August, 1955

Here I am in New Delhi,

in the Imperial Hotel. They've given me an extraordinary apartment, huge, with a living room and patio, and an Indian and Western bathroom joined into one.

Although I sent telegrams to Swami Sivananda from Baghdad and from Damascus and again from Pakistan, I don't think they ever arrived. A letter from a swami with an unpronounceable name said I would be met at the airport, but no one has come to meet me and there has been no word from the ashram. Fortunately, I met two Englishmen who told me that Caucasian women could not travel alone in India and suggested that I stay at the Imperial Hotel where they were registered. I have very little money, so I hope this apartment is not too costly. The Englishmen said they were paying 35 rupees—that's about $7.00.

An Austrian woman came in with linen to make the bed and we started a conversation. It is so good to talk to somebody in my own language. She told me her family had a little country hotel just outside Vienna. A few Indian men had stayed at their place and had asked her if she would come and organize a hotel in India where Westerners could be comfortable. They offered her a good salary so she accepted.

I asked her if she could help me get to Rishikesh, where the ashram is located. She suggested that I should phone the ashram. I tried for two hours without success.

When I unpacked I discovered that somehow I have forgotten to bring any dresses with me, so I have only the dress I'm wearing, a velvet rain coat, some pants, a couple of blouses and a pullover. The heat is around 110° F. It's too late to go shopping and anyway I'm too exhausted. I wonder what has happened? Why has nobody come to pick me up? I feel stranded and lost.

Lying stretched out on my bed

I was wondering about Swami Sivananda and trying to get over my feeling of being abandoned when I saw three lizards on the ceiling above me. I nearly collapsed. What if they should fall on my bed during the night—or worse, on my face? I got through the night somehow. In the morning my dress was damp from the humidity but I had to put it on. I went down to the hotel lobby and asked the manager where I could buy some clothes. He was most kind and accompanied me to a shop that was run by ladies only, and he made sure I would find my way back. There were no Western dresses, only saris. I chose three. I found I knew how to put on a sari without being shown, but there was still the problem of a slip and blouse. I decided that I would have to use my pyjama pants for the moment in place of a slip. One of the salesladies suggested that a Kashmiri blouse would do until I could have some made by a tailor. I took two Kashmiri blouses and then hurried back to the hotel. It has taken the rest of the day to arrange a booking on the train from New Delhi to Hardwar.

The very nice and helpful man from the hotel offered to go with me to the railway station to buy my ticket. He knew that Rishikesh was a town of swamis, saints, sadhus and holy men and he seemed to be impressed that anyone would come so far to meet these saints, who do not seem to get much attention any more. I changed some travellers checks at the cashier's office. He gave me bundles of one-rupee notes. By now I had become quite suspicious, since I had earlier paid $3.00 for a couple of bananas that should have cost me only 25¢. Fixed prices are unknown and everybody enjoys bargaining. Unfortunately I do not, so I stood at the counter until I had counted and made sure I had the right amount. I was 25 rupees short. The cashier smiled mischievously, as if it were a joke, but handed the missing money over. When I paid my hotel bill I got a shock. It was 100 rupees a day—$25.00. I protested that I had not asked for the suite of rooms, one bedroom would have done nicely, but this didn't help. It was a tremendous bite into the small reserves that I had brought to India.

With the help of a taxi driver who drove me to the station, I found my compartment. I had decided to travel first-class, since I could not take any more unpleasant surprises, but I did not know that I should have bought a ticket for the ladies' section. I discovered that I was to travel with two Indian men. Remembering the warning of the English gentlemen that Indians are very passionate and curious, I was worried. As I was struggling to get my luggage into the compartment, one of the gentlemen addressed me very politely. "Madam, do you know you have to share the compartment with us? We are both inspectors of the railway. Let us help you with your luggage and we will do what we can to make your journey pleasant."

I must have still looked concerned because the other inspector said, "Yes, I am an inspector too. Please feel comfortable and safe. We shall take the upper berths so you can have the lower." What I had considered benches to sit on turned out to be berths to sleep on. The two men climbed up and rolled out sleeping bags, which are called "hold-alls" in India because they are used for carrying clothes and other belongings.

I was too excited and too tired to be able to sleep. I thought from the map I had studied at the hotel that we would be in Hardwar in two hours. I was in for more surprises. The train was over an hour late in leaving, finally departing at about 9 o'clock. People were running alongside the train selling coffee, tea, cookies, and fruit, and the two railway inspectors proved to be very helpful getting some food for me. Naturally, I invited them to sit on the lower benches to eat. I wondered what would happen to the dishes, but they said the train would not leave until all the dishes were collected. I asked when we would be in Hardwar and they said probably between 3 and 4 in the morning. I couldn't understand why it would take so long. I soon found out. The train finally got under way but it stopped again in an hour. People came aboard, visited their friends and relatives, talked, and had something to eat. The dishes were collected again, people embraced and waved goodbye, and slowly the train pulled out.

It stopped a couple more times. By then I was getting too tired to check the time. The inspectors stretched out on their bunks and went to sleep. I used my coat and my newly acquired parcel for a mattress on the hard bench. Finally at 4 o'clock in the morning we arrived in Hardwar. The train inspectors suggested that, instead of waiting two and a half hours for the next train, I should take a taxi, since the distance was only a few miles. They would try to get one for me and within an hour I would be in Rishikesh. They figured out that I should pay 10 rupees after I arrived at my destination. I watched this bargaining and was amazed at how the inspector got the price down to half what the taxi driver had originally asked. The luggage was put in the car and off I went.

We drove through the sleeping little town of Hardwar and I was deeply shocked at what I saw. Most of the houses were in a dreadful state of dilapidation. They didn't look as if they had been painted or repaired since they were built. There didn't appear to be any proper sanitation facilities and the houses were so dirty that they almost made me shiver. Since modern transportation permits us to travel so fast from one country to another, the contrast between the East and the wealthy West is more marked and more surprising, because there is no time for gradual adjustment.

I was feeling very uneasy. The taxi was dusty, its torn upholstery covered with dirty blankets. The driver looked like a beggar. For the first time in my life I have come into contact with a completely different attitude toward life. I suddenly realize that we are all the product of our environment, even to the smallest detail. Points of view and opinions are dropped into us like coins into a machine. Of course, much of this has been done with the best intentions and is meant as preparation for life. Yet most of the difficulties in our lives are derived from these preconceived ideas.

As dawn began to break, we passed more and more miserable creatures along the road. They waved their hands, they smiled. I was deeply affected. I found myself thinking, what will the ashram be like? I dare not imagine. Suddenly we came to what looked like a rushing river flowing directly across the road. The driver stopped and indicated by gestures (he couldn't speak English) that we could not drive any further. A private car stopped beside us and the owner stepped out and came over to speak to me. He explained that although the monsoon season was coming to an end, last night there had been heavy rainfall which had resulted in flooding. After inspecting the situation, he turned his car around to seek another way. Two big trucks have stopped also and everyone is waiting. It looks hopeless. A good time to continue my diary.

I am trying to comfort myself by thinking of Sivananda. In geographic distance I have come very close to him, but in spirit he seems to be farther away than ever. I am so eager to meet this man who was able to project himself to me in Canada. How could he do this? There must be ways of communicating that we do not even perceive, let alone understand. Some of us occasionally become aware of their existence, but not everyone has this awareness. Why is this so? Mothers and wives experience something when a son or husband is killed and later receive the tragic confirmation of their intuitive knowledge. There is a very strong link between mother and child, husband and wife. This kind of link is the only explanation I can give of the communication between Swami Sivananda and me. Since childhood I have been aware of a sensitiveness, an extrasensory awareness, which brought occasionally happy, but most often sad, revelations. It was for me a mixed blessing, but it seems that through this sensitivity Sivananda and I were able to make contact.

Soon I will meet Sivananda. Surely he will protect the pupil who comes in confidence to him.

At this point, the driver indicated with gestures that I should get out of the car. He took out my luggage and put it on the road. I didn't know what to do. I thought again of Sivananda. Surely he will help somehow. I know I must stay here. Better to remain in the taxi.

* * * * *

Another hour has passed. My mind dwells on the book by Swami Sivananda, *Concentration and Meditation*. He speaks there of the need for a spiritual teacher and of the necessity for complete obedience by the pupil. I wonder how I will feel about this. As a child I was terribly spoiled and obedience was never really demanded from me. In our age of reason I do not think that anyone would demand blind obedience, although here in India, where they appear a hundred years behind, I'm not so sure. I'm not worried about hardships. The war was my great trainer and I know I can be indifferent to deprivation and plenty alike. For more than ten years in Berlin we were without proper food. Now, in spiritual practice, the fasting and many other exercises seem useless for me. Even my fear of death was lost in those terrible years of bombings, only the fear of becoming a cripple remained.

The driver has disappeared. I hope he is investigating the situation. Two hours have passed since we left Hardwar. God makes things very difficult for those who want to come to Him.

* * * * *

The driver has returned. Although the flood doesn't seem to have receded very much, he has put the luggage back and we are slowly driving through the water, making waves like a ship.

* * * * *

On the other side of the bridge he drove with tremendous speed as if trying to make up for lost time. More dirty and dilapidated houses. As I remember, in Germany poor families kept their homes and themselves neat and clean. Here people are dressed in rags, their skeleton-like bodies showing through the torn material. So this is India! We passed a building that looked like a temple, in very bad condition, as though it had not been used for years. *What is the ashram going to be like?*

Finally we stopped in front of a big sign "Sivanandanagar" (meaning "Sivananda's town"—the ashram is like a little town!). A pleasant swami in a flaring orange robe greeted me and arranged for my luggage to be carried up to a little cottage where I was to stay. At the cottage another swami, who told me his name was Paramananda, came to welcome me. He pointed to a large, low table by the wall and told me it was my bed. He opened a door to another room with a small tank in the corner filled with water. This was supposed to be the bathroom, but there was no toilet! How can I find out about such intimate things? From swamis? The walls were wet, which I assumed was fresh paint, but Swami Paramananda said no, it was condensation, the humidity from the monsoons. There is no chest of drawers, no closet—only an iron bar across the room for hanging my clothes on.

Swami Paramananda excused himself, saying he would come back with some tea and refreshments. Almost immediately there was a knock on the door and outside stood a thin gentleman, looking like a Biblical prophet with his white hair and beard. He introduced himself as Ayyapan and offered to be of any help he could. He showed me the veranda, which was covered with heavy chain wire to keep the monkeys and other animals out, where there was a table on which I placed the typewriter and some paper I had brought.

Ayyapan lives next door. He speaks English and seems to be well educated. He told me that he was a disciple of Swami Sivananda and had come to receive his Sannyas initiation from him. He wears the typical white cloth of the *brahmacharya* before becoming a *sannyasin* (a renunciate). Swami Paramananda came back with tea, black coffee, milk and sugar, cookies and a couple of bananas. He warned me about the monkeys, who will snatch food from your hand if they can, and are even able to open doors that are not properly latched.

After I had eaten, Swami Paramananda suggested I rest, but when Ayyapan invited me to take a little walk my curiosity overcame my fatigue and I accepted. He showed me around my cottage, which is called a *kutir*, and pointed out how important it is to close the doors properly because the monkeys are very clever and will come in if given the slightest opportunity. Whenever my eyes fell on a door, I asked him where it led, wondering if it might be a ladies room.

He told me that everyone is addressed as Swamiji, which I find very confusing, except that when they speak of Big Swami they always mean Swami Sivananda—"your guru," Ayyapan said to me. He continued, "You came at a very good time. The great heat is over now and winter is very pleasant. I guess it will be as it is in your country." The great heat is over? The temperature is 102° in the shade!

Swami Paramananda came back and said, "Your guru wants to meet you!" Surprisingly, I realized I was not excited. Neither had I been excited at the prospect of going to India before I left Montreal. Maybe from the time I stepped off the plane in New Delhi I have been too overwhelmed with the strangeness of it all to feel excited. Now I am about to meet India's greatest saint and still there is no excitement.

The office was packed with people. We made our way through the bookstore to a door leading to the office of the Master. Here I

Sylvia Hellman practising meditation on the roof
of her apartment in Canada.

had my first look at Sivananda, who was sitting in front of the window so that he appeared in silhouette. Through the middle of the room ran what appeared to be a small wooden platform on which we had to weave our way through the people who packed the place. I was carrying my heavy tape recorder and the gifts I had brought for Swami Sivananda—a velvet box containing a cross and a cumbersome parcel of material to be made into a coat for him. Thus burdened, it was very difficult to balance on this narrow plank and move through the crowded room. I couldn't see where I was walking. My foot slipped and I fell into the crowd. With surprising calm I picked myself up and went toward Sivananda.

Standing in front of the Master there was still no excitement. He was so familiar to me. I thought of Sivananda's words when he had invited me to come, "Here is your real home. I will share with you what I have. Spiritual wealth. . ." I remember in Canada once when I was meditating on him, his presence was so real that I felt like someone who had been away for a long time. I felt his hand gently caressing my hair and his voice, as now, comforting me, "Don't cry. Now you are here again, everything is all right. You have come home now." Then I realized it was because we had met before that there was no excitement.

"You come from America?" he asked. "From Canada," I replied. He offered me a chair in front of his huge desk. Then I handed him the blue velvet box containing the cross, my gift for him. He could not find the spring to open it, so I did it for him. With the cross in his hands, he said smilingly, "Now I am one with Canada and America."

He tried to open the lock on the chain, but his hands were too big and again I took it from him, opened the lock, and put the cross around his neck. Not for a moment did my hands shake. It was as though we were continuing from where we had left off yesterday. He wore the cross all day—I think it was a wonderful gesture indicating that he, the Hindu saint, was ready to show his respect for another religion by wearing its symbol.

"You like tea or coffee?" Sivananda asked. Before I could say anything he answered himself, "She likes coffee." "I have given up coffee," I said in a low voice. "Yes, yes, that is why you can drink coffee again," and he had a swami bring me coffee. He dealt with the many papers in front of him, signing, making notes and then handing them back to his swami assistants.

I was feeling very dirty and untidy and he seemed to become aware of this. He said something to Swami Paramananda, who took me back to my little cottage, saying, "You will find warm water for a bath. And you can have some time for yourself." That was what I needed. I still had not found a toilet. Too shy to ask, I made my way into the bush which I found must have been the place everyone used. I bathed and put on a sari.

After lunch, which came on a tray, Swami Paramananda took me to the roof of a huge building where Swami Sivananda was seated in a comfortable chair and the others sat crosslegged on carpets in front of him. He smiled at me, "You look like an Indian lady. The sari suits you beautifully." A swami came with a camera and took pictures. I was to pose for a picture with Swami Sivananda, so we went down to the banks of the Ganges where he put some garlands around my neck. He moved freely and naturally, not as one would expect the great admired guru of India to behave, the one to whom Indians bow down so deeply that their heads touch the ground. I felt at ease with him, free and very happy. After the pictures, we joined the group again. A young Indian girl caressed my feet gently and put one of her rings on my toe. The Master noticed and smiled, "You make friends quickly."

I looked around me at the colorful scene. Men in long robes with wavy hair and wild-looking beards; women in colorful saris decorated with all sorts of ornaments. Some had jewels in their nostrils, rings on their toes and bangles on their wrists. Not only the women, but also some men had outlined their eyes in black. The appearance of a sophisticated Western woman would seem quite drab compared to that of these Indian women with their many-colored decorations and ornate jewelry. I felt as though I

The entrance arch at Sivananda Ashram, Rishikesh, India.
"I felt as though I were transported to Biblical times."

were transported to Biblical times. The salutation to the Master reminded me of the footwashings of Jesus by His disciples and the women around Him. I felt as though I were dreaming and yet it all seemed so familiar.

Another memory flooded back. Once in Montreal when I was pressed to attend a social gathering, I had to miss my usual meditation. I was engaged in what I now consider empty conversation. Suddenly Sivananda appeared as in that first meditation, took my hand and said, "Why do you waste precious time?" and together we seemed to move to some higher plane.

My eyes wandered back to him. Did he know? Or was all this only a trick of my own mind?

2 September

My first night in the ashram!

What a night! To begin with, this thing I'm supposed to sleep on looks and feels more like a table than a bed. There are only two very thin blankets of poor quality. I folded one in four parts as some protection for my poor bones on the unyielding board. The second blanket served as a cover and I rolled up my coat for a pillow. I had finally stretched myself out and was attempting to find a position comfortable enough for sleep when I was startled by a scream. I rushed into the bathroom and found another Western girl who lives in the next room staring at a spider the size of a dinner plate. Ayyapan, also awakened by the scream, came running in and chased the spider down the drain. The rest of the night passed somehow in a turmoil of dreams about spiders, lizards, bedbugs and everything that can crawl. Will I ever get used to this?

There is hardly a book which does not tell the aspirant that the early morning hour is the best for meditation and other spiritual pursuits. Shortly before 5 o'clock my alarm rang. It needed all my effort to get up because of the sleepless nights I have had since I left Canada. The reward was the wonderful experience of seeing the dawn—the sun rising over the foothills of the Himalayas. The Ganges glittered between the green leaves of the trees and on the other shore I could see the little temple of Swarg Ashram where, I am told, Swami Sivananda spent 12 years in spiritual practice (tapas).

5 September

I **have now been at the ashram** for four days and my life has settled down to a certain routine. My body's rebellion against the discomfort of my table-bed is lessening. I cannot imagine I shall ever adjust to the food nor to the lack of cleanliness and sanitation. The bugs continue to be a great trial to me. At times I can scarcely find a spot on my body that is not bitten. The monkeys I enjoy—mischievous, clever, thieving, but quite disarming.

Yesterday I was talking to Mr. Radner, a European who has lived here for a few years writing his books. His wife visits him from time to time with the children. He showed me a copy of *Divine Life,* a magazine printed as a birthday edition in honor of Swami Sivananda. There are articles and letters giving thanks to the Master for the kindness he has shown to many people. Once their troubles are over, people often forget the help they received, but in these writings the expression of love and devotion was really touching.

Mr. Radner, however, saw these letters only as an overflow of emotions by hysterical people wanting to get the great Master's attention. "Just look at this." He pointed to a page with the title, "My angelic Master," from a woman in Canada. "I am sure she is just another one dissatisfied with her husband and now she throws herself into the Master's lap. These Westerners, especially women, seem to be not only fascinated but hypnotized by every thing that is Indian."

I picked up the magazine and read my own name! It was a condensation of several of my letters written before coming to the ashram. I am shocked and upset that things were disclosed to the public which were meant for the Master only. I had written out of gratitude for the spiritual help he had given me, but now, as I read my words condensed into one letter, they really sound ridiculous. I have become aware of a pride existing in me, a pride I did not know I had. I had *not* been asked for permission. I am amazed that Sivananda consents to such things.

* * * * *

I asked Sivananda about publishing my letters. He said, "I will reprint all your letters and lectures as they will help others who are on the same level as you are." I find this very difficult. I suppose it is true that highly philosophical books cannot help in times of despair, while an account by someone who has gone through the same deep pain that all God seekers have in common (be they Indian or Western) may bring solace and encouragement. With evolving awareness of pride, one discovers how the mind deceives to an extent one had not even dreamed of before. I suppose this goes on until the state of highest realization is reached. We find examples of this among the lives of Christian saints. They confess that they are the greatest sinners because they have become aware of the tricks of the mind, the subtleness of the ego and the working of the Divine Law.

* * * * *

Satsang is unknown in the West, and here at the ashram it is a totally new experience for me. It takes place at night in a sort of tent, but not enclosed. We can see the dark tropical heavens glimmering with stars. The Milky Way is directly above us, the hills form a black silhouette, and the rushing Ganges reflects the moon.

Watching all the people gathered around the Master last night I found myself thinking that in this place an observer with an open mind could study the full range of development from high spirituality right down to disgusting selfishness. The question of how much free will man really has becomes more and more significant when one sees so many people driven by their vanity and greed. The orange robe does not seem to be any protection from the stirring of the lower instincts. Among the great number of people, I should think there are only about nine swamis on whose sincerity, modesty and ability the Master can really count. Perhaps one who seems sincere today will desert the guru tomorrow, in search of faster enlightenment, or will yield unexpectedly to the dictates of his lower self. This frightens me, that there seem to be no heights so great that one is safe from falling. Even Jesus was tempted—He, the Son of God. What is this dangerous thing I have got myself into? Yet I cannot leave it. I seem to be driven.

6 September

A *woman who introduced herself as Lila*

has succeeded in disturbing my peace of mind. She said, "You came all the way from Canada to find your guru in Sivananda? Poor woman, you probably had to work hard to save enough money to come all this distance and now you will be disappointed. He is a nice man, yes, but no saint, no guru. You will find out."

I felt sick. "I must wash and change my clothes," I said, to get rid of her. After she left I tried to shake off the feeling of doubt she had raised. Why? Am I not sure? Is everything a hallucination? There must be some people who surely have become aware of Sivananda's saintliness and greatness as a guru.

In the afternoon Lila repeated her visit. She tried to comfort me by promising that she would take me to a *real* guru. She described his powers, some of which she claimed to have witnessed. I felt empty, lost in a kind of vacuum. Of course, it is not unusual for a saint to be unrecognized in his own country. Did not Jesus experience this? But I can't think clearly because it involves much more than the question of whether or not Swami Sivananda is a guru or a real saint. The important question is, are prayers answered? Is he or is he not the answer to my intense prayers?

This God, Divine Power, or Cosmic Energy seems to be something of indescribable cruelty, making one's heart ache, one's mind the battlefield of numerous conflicting thoughts. Even the thought that Christ Himself said, "My God, why have you forsaken me?" does not bring any relief. The whole ashram suddenly appears to be nothing more than a marionette theatre and he—God or Guru—pulls the string. The stupid marionettes only fool themselves in thinking that they do something on their own.

Now everything seems ten times more difficult—the food cooked with such hot spices that I cannot eat it. The cold potatoes, bananas and oranges have no appeal for me tonight either, because of my state of deep inner despair. All the *whys* are coming back—why creation? Life is not worth living. The price for every happy hour is much too great. The hope that in Sivananda I have found one who has attained Realization is diminishing.

7 *September*

Another beautiful day.

I am feeling happier today, as though expressing my doubts has given them less strength. The monkeys with their little black faces framed by a white circle of fur are so entertaining they make me forget my sorrow. I have been writing letters, sitting on my veranda where the view is beautiful. I seem to make an inner contact with my correspondents; my answers flow from the heart.

* * * * *

As usual, Swami Paramananda, whom I think of as "The Foreign Minister" because he looks after the foreign visitors, took me to the office where Swami Sivananda was working. Sometimes Master would ask a question jokingly, sometimes seriously. Sometimes he would drop his pen and glasses and start chanting *Om* and other Sanskrit prayers and everyone would join him. He looked at me.

"Who is the biggest surgeon?" he asked. Then when I remained silent, fearing a trick because of the mischievous smile on his face, he answered himself, "God. God is the greatest surgeon. He operates on the ego daily." We all laughed.

After a little while he asked me, "Who are you?" I smiled at him. "Sivananda, thy own Self." He often signed his letters to me "Thy own Self—Thy own Atman Siva," as a reminder that I should not identify with the body but realize the divine spirit in myself and in him and be aware of the oneness with all.

* * * * *

In his first letter inviting me to the ashram, Sivananda offered to give me an opportunity to study Bharata Natyam dancing. Only afterwards did I admit that I was really a professional dancer. Today Swami Venkatesananda came to me and said, "The Master wants to see you dance."

"I will rehearse," I answered, "and then find out about costumes and music."

"The Master wants to see you now." Swamiji made the point quite clear.

"But I have to rehearse, find proper music. I cannot dance on this carpet, all wrinkled up, and watch out for all the babies to see that I don't step on them. Besides, if he wants to see Indian dancing, I am not an expert and I have no anklebells for the timing." I was so surprised. I could hardly believe that anybody could expect me to dance without any preparation.

"Music is here, you can listen," Swamiji said, "and bells I will get for you. You are not going to refuse the very first wish of your guru?"

"You are not going to refuse the very first wish of your guru?
I danced for Sivananda."

What could I say? When he returned with the anklebells, the battle with my pride was over—my pride as a dancer and artist, my reputation, the fear of criticism I would receive if I did not do well. All vanished.

I danced for Sivananda. I did not step on babies, I did not fall over the wrinkles of the carpet, I did not even lose the beat in spite of the drummer, who was so surprised that he forgot to drum and simply stared at me. I danced and narrated an old Indian prayer for which I have always had a great liking.

When I had finished, I went over to the Master and gave my *pranam,* or bow, as I had seen it done by other people. I said, "I'm sorry if you are disappointed." But he was all smiles. "Oh no, that was all right. Now do another dance, not Indian." I tried to excuse myself on the grounds that I could not have appropriate music, but he did not accept this. Finally I agreed to do a Persian dance. "But," I said, "I must have a veil." At once he removed from his neck a piece of veil-like cotton and handed it to me. So I could not deny him.

I am becoming more and more aware that once you are in his net you cannot escape him. He is a great fisherman and in his net of spirituality he brings people to the Divine.

8 *September*

Tonight Sivananda picked up pieces

of clothing from people around him, decorated himself and began dancing. His heavy body showed surprising lightness and the gracefulness of his hands appeared almost feminine. I was amazed. His high spirits swept everyone off their feet in a kind of divine ecstasy. This is his 69th birthday, 8 September, 1955, and hundreds and hundreds of people have come to celebrate the occasion from all over the world as well as all over India. He seems to have the strength to carry everyone along with him.

There were musicians but few that appealed to my Western ears. Because of the expanded scale of Eastern music, it sounds to us as though they are out of tune. There was a blind man and his wife who had very pleasant voices, compared to others who seemed only to scream. My hypersensitivity to noise means that it becomes unbearable to listen for several hours at a stretch. My nerves become so tense that my whole body is affected and the usual pain in my spine seems to double.

Somebody started to play the veena and I began to relax. The sound of the veena has a strange effect on me, as I had already discovered in Canada. After about half an hour I would experience a strange state of mind, very relaxed, almost hypnotic. It would be worthwhile to study the human reaction to sound. I was told by my father that as a small baby I closed my little ears with my hands when there was an unpleasant sound. It is known that some sounds can cause certain feelings in a human being, but much in this field is left to be discovered. We know so little about our inner nature, yet we try so hard to find out about other things, particularly ways to improve our physical comfort and convenience. Why don't we put more effort into self-discovery?

Later, though satsang was still going on, the "Foreign Minister," like a good father, took me back to my little cottage where he arranged for food and rest. This gentle yet dynamic man lives for his guru only. To be Swami Paramananda's friend, one must be true and obedient to the Master. He is Gurudev's watchdog, who helps keep the importunate devotees from overtiring him. Strangely enough, people who claim to be spiritual seekers can be so greedy, they don't care what it costs the Master as long as their emotional longing is fulfilled.

It is simply terrible that my

Western habits make me so demanding, but Swami Paramananda does everything to make things as easy as possible. Often he seems to know in advance what I need and he is kind enough not to make me beg for things that must appear to him absolutely unnecessary.

The word has got around about the visitor from Canada. As many as 30 people have come up to my veranda, one by one, to talk to me. Several of them told me that if I believed Swami Sivananda to be a great guru, I was mistaken. I was stunned. I asked them why they came to the ashram then. "Oh, we just have cheap holidays and Swami Sivananda gives shelter to all, without questioning why we come." This frankness amazed me. Some of the people pitied me and tried to comfort me, suggesting I visit some other gurus.

I was greatly disturbed. Sometimes we want to believe in something and we will turn and twist everything to fit our need to believe. I felt as though I had been thrown from the crest of the wave and had crashed on the sand and stones. This mental pain became so great that my physical pain from sleeping on the hard board seemed as nothing.

Swami Paramananda noticed my depression and tried to cheer me up. I desperately laid my questions before him. He answered with such simplicity and conviction that I had to listen to him. He said, "I do not know myself about the powers of Swami Sivananda. I have stayed with him for 25 years because of his greatness, his kindness. I have not found this greatness and kindness to the same extent in any other person. Because I have observed only good in him, I have dedicated my life to him." This simple statement was more helpful than if he had tried with all the power of his personality to impose his beliefs on me. And I have learned from this that doubt is very necessary. Doubt leads to the discovery of knowledge and to truth. "I believe" means "I don't know." When one knows, one does not need to believe.

10 September

Again this morning Master as usual

offered me the chair in front of his desk in the office. Occasionally he would hand me a book or pamphlet or offer me an Indian sweet (called *prasad*, since it has been blessed by a saint). I was observing everything with my critical mind. People came saluting him, bowing down to his feet. He looked bored. He looked bored all the time during satsang. He looked bored when people performed *Pada Puja*, the worship of the feet of the guru. If he feels bored, why does he submit to these things? Fame? He was a physician before he became a guru, he could have become a famous doctor if he had wanted that. Money? He had had plenty of it and independence on top of that. How can people feel inspired or uplifted during this worship when he does not give them a single glance but keeps on attending to the swamis coming and going, handing him papers, asking for his signature? Surely this business is not so important that it couldn't wait for an hour or so. Looking after the physical needs of these people is not enough. Does he not know that the mental anguish is many times more intense than any physical pain? Oh, why must I have this restless mind, always probing, never satisfied?

In the afternoon, Ayyapan invited me to take a walk. We went toward Lakshmanjula where I was amused by the notice board on the suspension bridge: "Elephants, camels and automobiles are forbidden."

There were a number of beggars lined up, most of them crippled, blind or old. Ayyapan explained to me that many of them have been crippled as a result of that terrible sickness, leprosy. Some years ago the Master, assisted by his swamis, nursed lepers with no fear for his own health. When the ashram could no longer accommodate the great number who came, a colony was founded a few miles away on a piece of land big enough to hold a little hut for each. In time the government took over and appointed a doctor who now stays permanently in the colony. But Master and the swamis still look after the spiritual and certain of the physical needs of these unfortunate people by arranging kirtans (chanting sessions) and by distributing blankets and clothing. Science still has not found a cure nor the cause of this terrible disease, nor has it been established whether it is contagious. Children often remain unaffected in spite of living with their afflicted parents. You would think that diseased parents would arrange for their children to be looked after by someone else, in case it is infectious, yet it seems that the parents would rather risk the health of their children than give them up. What kind of love is that? Really, it is only attachment. Yet the love of a mother is supposed to be the most perfect human love. It seems there is perfection nowhere. Is it possible to find a love that asks nothing in return? Could we even understand such love?

In spite of never having experienced it, we still seek perfection in others, especially in a religious person. Yet I suppose that even a saint has limitations. As awareness expands, one discovers the subtle obstacles that block the way to perfection. But it is very dangerous to judge others, especially great spiritual souls. How can anyone become aware of the subtle workings within saints? Only they know what their mission is, what they have to do. No other person can know.

Where are these thoughts leading me? What is the purpose? To "find God"? A child does not need to go in search of its mother. Why do we have these uncertainties about God?

All the human attributes we give God can comfort us only as

long as we remain confined by the perceptions of the mind. Our only hope is to try with all possible effort to expand these limitations. Scientists tell us that our globe is but a speck among millions of other specks in the universe, so we should be under no illusion as to our importance. But even our limited faculties are given to us for some purpose. We as individuals must have some value. Every single cell of my body exists without being consciously experienced every moment and yet it belongs to the whole. Without the body it has no existence of its own. And this body is only a cell of something bigger—we are a part of something important. I wonder if this is how we can make the transition from nothingness to Oneness. But this does not still the hunger for the highest. What is this highest I am longing for? I don't know myself—only that I can't escape it.

12 September

Meditation at 4 or 5 o'clock

in the morning is still difficult for me in spite of the beautiful surroundings of the Himalayas, the Ganges and the general atmosphere of peace and serenity. Even with the refreshing quietness, the thoughts in my mind run wild. Strange. In Canada, in the turmoil of a big city I had less difficulty concentrating. Why? Is it because of my doubts about Swami Sivananda that burn my inner being, giving me no rest? The Himalayas, dark silhouettes against the lightening sky, are the dividing line between darkness and light. It seems I must remain in the darkness until I find the Truth.

No religion can claim a monopoly on Truth. Everyone has his own incomplete interpretation of God. Imagine God as nothing more and nothing less than the total of all existing energy in the cosmos? Only in that way can I think of God. But I must admit it is tremendously difficult to build any inner relationship, by means of prayer or similar practice, to such *neutral energy*. Maybe the old picture of a personal God with which I was infused as a child is still there, even although I don't accept it. Maybe one cannot reject an old idea completely before understanding and absorbing the new one.

16 September

I am no scholar — I have done little

to improve my academic knowledge since leaving boarding school at the age of 18. But I was born with a very inquisitive mind and this has been driving me since I was a little girl. Life without truth and purpose is meaningless, and I would rather be with truth in hell than in heaven with illusions.

Many *sadhus* come to the ashram, their bodies covered with ashes, their faces painted with different colors, indicating in what aspect they worship God. These *sadhus* live by old tradition. What does that mean? Tradition alone is no answer. If Christ is right that by the fruits you will recognize the tree, then many trees must be dead. The spirituality in India appears to belong to the past. How will the Hindus convince us of their spiritual truth, unable as they are to solve their own problems?

There is a handful of spiritual people in every country. I am convinced that Western monasteries house some spiritual giants, unadvertised. The prayers of these men and women are as powerful in the quietude of their monasteries as the prayers of a *sadhu* in the solitude of the Himalayas. Life in a cave is most impressive— the most perfect renunciation. But for whom? Someone who has never tasted the comforts of life in the West? One who walks from babyhood without shoes does not find them difficult to give up. Perhaps I am unjust. Why all these negative thoughts? It would be far more beautiful to fulfill the expectations and illusions with which I came here. Are my preconceived ideas the basis for an illusion that has no reality? I came with hopes for the personal guidance I think is essential to prevent disaster; are they unrealistic? If Sivananda cannot give me that guidance, who can?

17 September

Swami Sadasivananda

just came back from his bath in the Ganges. I had to stop him to see if he could help me with my confusion. Swamiji listened attentively, became very serious and said, "I will tell you a story in which lies the answer.

"A king and a merchant had retired into the forest. Each one had built a hut for himself in a different place along the same path. To each Divine Providence appeared in the form of a messenger. He first came to the king with a large tray on which there were six or seven different types of food. He returned with a smaller tray carrying only three different types of food. The merchant said, 'Why do I get less? Is there no justice?' The messenger looked at him sternly and said, 'The king has renounced more.' Then he turned and left."

Swamiji did the same. I took the symbols of the story apart, as I had already learned from interpreting dreams, to try to decipher the message. One part was obvious—the king had renounced more than the merchant, so each one received according to the degree of his renunciation.

Both were in the forest. In the forest one cannot see far; the trees block vision. This indicated that there was ignorance in both of them and inner vision had not yet been obtained. Yet their huts, their place to live, they had to build for themselves on the same path. Each built according to his desire, or was it needs? How does one get out of the forest of confused thinking? How does one achieve clear vision?

19 *September*

I missed the sunrise this morning.

Sleep kept me prisoner. I am up too late at night. The changes are too many and too great and take a tremendous amount of energy. My few hours of sleep are ruined by the bedbugs. I miss the hygiene and simple cleanliness to which I am accustomed. Sitting on the floor crosslegged for four hours of satsang is torture. After a while the delightful and inspiring music becomes a strain and grates on my ears. Sitting as close as possible to Sivananda in order not to miss anything he says is some consolation to me.

Food has become more and more of a problem for me at the ashram. It is so spicy it is impossible for me to eat it, not only because it is too hot for my mouth but also because my body rebels. Today I bought at the bazaar a tin of cheese, a tin of butter, bananas and oranges, but this is very expensive. Gurudev often gives me large tins of English biscuits, but these do not replace a proper meal. In Sivananda's books he says there should be no spices, no catering to taste, and yet the hottest food I have ever had in my life is served here at the ashram. Gurudev himself eats the hottest chilies; and he has diabetes. Why does he not adhere to his own precepts? Simple meals could be made with the food available here at the ashram.

The cup of milk I get at satsang from Sivananda gives me some nourishment, but I have found that these cups are never properly washed. One day I discovered that a little orphan boy rinsed them in a tiny pail, pouring the water from one cup to another, and there were about 20 cups. Then he left them on the ground. So the stray dogs come around and lick them—and they also lick their sores and boils. Besides, I have been warned by Mr. Radner, the journalist who lives at the ashram, not to drink any milk at all because the cows have T.B.

* * * * *

I am baffled more and more by the workings of the Indian mind. Today when returning from the bazaar I found a message pinned on my door. It read, "Swami Sivananda wants you immediately to come to his kutir." Eagerly I walked over to him and he said, "I have special food for you." One of the swamis with him uncovered a plate that held a beautiful pancake. For weeks I have not had a proper meal, so I was delighted. Master had a mischievous smile on his face as he said, "Eat it, eat it." I took a bite of the pancake, which was covered with a layer of sugar. No sooner had the sugar melted in my mouth than I could hardly breathe. I coughed and choked for several minutes. Then I realized that Gurudev and the swamis were laughing their heads off. This is their idea of a joke! I am furious! Gurudev knows how spiced food upsets me. This is a bit more than I am willing to make an effort to understand. I feel like turning on my heel and leaving. By exercising the utmost discipline I managed to excuse myself politely and left. Gurudev is obviously not pleased with my reaction. But I also am not pleased. I cannot see what all this has to do with spirituality.

This morning Swami Paramananda

invited me to his kutir and showed me an enormous file of hand-written letters. "These are all Swami Sivananda's letters," he said, not without pride. "Now they are serving me in my correspondence with the Western people." I was shocked. Someone called him to the door at that moment and so gave me an excuse to leave.

Swamiji writes Sivananda's letters! Sivananda only signs them—he doesn't even read most of them! I realize that hundreds of letters come every day and he cannot look after so many. But why not tell people that he has a number of disciples who look after his correspondence but that he adds his blessing? I am at a loss. I am beginning to understand how many people find nothing remarkable about him except perhaps his generosity. But I didn't come 10,000 miles for oranges, saris, coffee, sweets. Holidays can be spent much more comfortably in other places, just as beautiful. I think there are other visitors here who are fighting their disappointment as much as I am, but they try to think up some sort of an explanation. Mr. Phillips, for instance, desperately wants some kind of experience with the great Master and is ready to construct anything, because he needs a guru for his plans after returning home. So he can't accept Sivananda as an ordinary human being.

I took out all my letters from Swami Sivananda and read them again. In the very first one he wrote, "I have been in seclusion for some time. I do not attend to any office work. I take delight in serving others. I will serve you nicely. Yes, you can take me as your guru. I will help you, guide you. Do not be bitter, looking back over your life, the Lord has prepared the field for a higher mission. Come and stay with me, here is your real home. I will share with you all I have—spiritual wealth, and I will provide you with room and food. I will train you personally in Yoga, delivering lectures, writing articles. I will send you the world over for dissemination of knowledge. You can learn Indian dancing here too." (This last sentence is most puzzling. I am absolutely certain I did not write a line about dancing.) I feel miserable. The letter is signed, "Thy own Self Sivananda."

Is this the answer to my prayers for someone to help me to become one with God? And yet I must remember again that Christ said, "If anyone of yourselves is asked by his son for bread, will he give him a stone? If he is asked for a fish, will he give him a serpent instead? Why, then, if you, evil as you are, know well enough how to give your children what is good for them, is not your Father in Heaven much more ready to give wholesome gifts to those who ask Him?" Crying won't help, the pain is too deep.

22 September

Swami Paramananda told me that
after lunch I could have an interview with Master and that he would answer questions. When I went to his kutir I was offered a comfortable seat on a sofa and served coffee with biscuits. Gurudev saw in my hands the paper on which I had written my questions.

"What is that?" he asked.

"Some questions." And I began reading the first.

"What is the next?" I read the second. "Give the paper to me. I will answer them all."

I said, "I would like to make a copy first." But he waved his hand, I was dismissed.

Why, I thought, does he invite people if he has no time? At the door he called me back. "Practice meditation. Go to the Dattatraya Temple. Wonderful place. Five o'clock is a good time. Start today."

Shortly before 5 this afternoon, I climbed up to the Dattatraya

Temple—Ayyapan had previously shown me where it was. I took a seat on the little bench, did a few pranayamas which I had learned in the Hatha Yoga class as preparation for meditation. I watched the black-faced monkeys playing in the trees for a little while and then I closed my eyes. Slowly my ear began to distinguish certain noises. I recognized the sound of monkeys jumping from tree to tree. Then I heard a strange sound, twigs cracking under the weight of a heavy animal. My imagination immediately took hold and presented the most terrifying possibilities. Didn't Lila tell me the other day that a tiger had got a calf while the ashramites were celebrating satsang? There must be all sorts of fierce wild animals here, with the jungle so close. Is this to be the end of it all for me? I've just arrived here—I've hardly learned anything yet.

My heart beat like a sledgehammer. I could feel warm air on my neck and ear. I did not dare to open my eyes. I was petrified with fear. When, after what seemed like an eternity, nothing had happened, I slowly forced my eyes open. A cow was trying to lick my face!

23 September

Today on my way to Master's kutir

a little monkey came begging for food. I had some food in my bag and gave him a bit. He started to gobble it up, looking nervously around in case a stronger monkey was coming to take the food from him. He tried to stuff his cheek pockets with as much as he could. Sure enough, a big fellow came along and frightened him away. I took out a little more food and put it in another place for the young monkey. When the old monkey saw it, he left the food he was greedily stuffing into himself to come over and get this new lot. At first I thought it was very funny and I couldn't help laughing, but now I am in the habit of reflecting on the events around me and I compared the monkey to human beings. Even when people have sufficient for their needs, they will take all they can get in their greediness, without consideration for the needs of others. There seems to be no end to greed.

I think I begin to understand why *sannyasins* are called "gods on earth." They have made a decision to search for the purpose of life and are prepared to renounce everything including their greed—to concentrate on the higher values in life. While many of Gurudev's initiates are not gods by my understanding of the term, I do see what he means and I also see how hard everyone is trying.

I do not know what expression I had on my face when I arrived at Gurudev's kutir, but his first remark was, "What is the monkey mind doing?"

Everybody laughed, and I did too, and I told them about feeding the monkeys, concluding by saying, "People who are greedy are ambitious. But how can anybody accomplish anything without being ambitious?" I took a deep breath and said to Master, "Are you ambitious for a big ashram?"

A swami stepped in front of me and said, "This is not the way to talk to the Master."

But Gurudev waved him aside and said, "Never mind, she wants to know. She is burning fire. I like that."

With a smile he turned to me, "Yes, I am ambitious. You are right. I am ambitious to be God's servant and do as much work for Him as I can and for all those that you see here. If I can help only one towards liberation, I have done my job."

I said, "So the difference is only where we place our ambition?"

The Master answered, "Yes, instead of having a monetary bank account, you are building up a spiritual bank account. Money is power, but so are prayers, mantras, all spiritual practice."

He stopped, but his eyes were still fixed on me. "You were bound to come to India. Because we have lived and worked together you were bound to come. You will be His servant." Again he paused. Then, "You can also be God's child. Choose whichever you like best. A mother already has milk for the baby before it is born."

Then he moved into his office. We all followed and I was about to make notes in the notebook he gave me when he said, "Notes are very good, but you must learn to listen with the heart, listen with intuition."

24 September

Lila asked me to go for a walk.

I was not much inclined but could not think of a good reason to refuse. She could disturb my peace of mind. I agreed because I wanted to overcome her negative influence on me. In spite of my positive attitude I'm afraid she did again shake me.

She told me about a pandit who visited the ashram one night and who gave a talk praising Western people and criticising the Indians, his own countrymen.

"What did Gurudev say?" I asked.

"He didn't say anything, but you should have seen his face, very cool and stern. He certainly didn't like it. In fact he killed the pandit."

I was amazed. "Killed? A guru never kills."

"Oh yes," she said, "For no reason at all the pandit suddenly complained of heart trouble and died a few days later."

I could not believe that. "How could he do such a thing? A nice old gentleman, a friend to humanity. And by what power could he do it?"

She said, "By some strange yogic power."

"But Lila, you told me yourself, he is nothing more than a nice old man, no guru, no master. Now you claim he has great yogic power, so much so that he can even kill at will."

"You will find out for yourself," she said and changed the subject, suggesting we have tea together.

This is a very upsetting situation and I would have preferred to refuse her invitation. Then I thought maybe her contradictions could help me deal with the doubts which she has created. As she kept talking it became obvious that such doubts, which are not the outcome of proper investigation, are not healthy. They are a poison that can be absorbed if one is not careful.

As she passed me tea and biscuits, she went on: "You think you came to get his help, but I say you came for his sake, not for your own."

"But Lila," I objected, "Why should he need me?" I could not help laughing at this.

"You must meet an Indian fellow, I don't know his name, I call him the major because he told me that he had formerly been with the Indian army and retired as a major. He lives in another ashram nearby, I think, because he comes very often to satsang over here. Now, since you have been here, he comes every night. He had already told me about you some months ago."

I was amused. It began to take on the shape of a grade B movie.

"This major," Lila continued, "knows you very well. His guru had shown you to him in his meditation and predicted that there would come a lady from across the sea who would bring a present to Swami Sivananda in the form of the sign of Christianity. When you got out of the taxi, we saw you from the top of the hill and he said, 'That is she, the small dark-haired one.' Would you mind telling me what made you bring the cross?"

"Not at all," I said. "I had become aware that one should bring a gift to the Master according to the Indian custom. I could not bring flowers or fruit, as they would spoil on the plane. I thought I must not come empty-handed, so I wracked my brain and finally got the idea of the cross. From his books and letters to me, I had the impression that he laid great stress on the unity of all religions, and therefore a cross seemed the right thing. From photographs I judged him to be very tall, so the cross must not be too

Speaking at satsang. "You're not going to talk from the level of your mind. Let the Divine flow through, just surrender." I obeyed.

small. I searched all over Montreal and finally discovered this one, but it was priced so high that it was out of the question.

"A few days before I left to come here, I passed the store again and the price had come down one hundred dollars. I immediately went into the store and wrote a check, leaving it for the weekend so that the storekeeper could make sure that my check was good and there was no mistake in the price. Then I picked it up on Monday and on Saturday took the plane for India. There is nothing mysterious about it except the providential reduction in the price."

"That is all in the Divine plan," Lila assured me. "Later on you will understand many things."

Then she said, "I will arrange for you to meet a *real* master. For the last thirty years he has lived in a cave about 16 miles from here. If he blesses you (which he may do with such force it will nearly knock you down) you will know the true purpose of your coming here."

Then I returned to my kutir and wondered, what *is* the real reason that I came to India?

25 September

Yesterday Master asked me to give

a talk. He said I should think about it and could make the choice of my theme, then tell him what I had decided. Last night I told him my subject and then typed out four or five pages so I could read it easily and make a good presentation.

Tonight at satsang I went up to Gurudev to get his blessing before giving the talk. He said, "Oh, the talk. Yes. And what have you there?" I handed him my speech. "Oh, yes, interesting. You have been very industrious. Excellent. Well, now you may go and give your talk." I asked for my papers back. "Oh, no, that is enough preparation. You're not going to talk from the level of your mind. Let the Divine flow through, just surrender."

I was stunned. I didn't know what to do. But there were about 300 people waiting for me to speak, so I spoke — not what I'd written on the paper. I don't know where the words came from, but they did flow after my first few moments of nervousness. I suppose that was another lesson in surrender.

26 September

There is no Western institution

to which the ashram could be compared. Catholic monasteries all over the world are established for the purpose of attaining God-consciousness by means of perfect discipline. This is carried out in the small details of everyday life, in complete obedience, punctuality, cleanliness, tidiness, orderliness. On such a foundation, in time, will be laid the spiritual discipline. Not so here in the ashram. Individuals have to make all the effort for themselves. In fact, there is no discipline at all — everybody interrupts everybody, even when talking to the Master. There seems to be no system in the work and it must be only by daily miracles that Sivananda's books are completed and go to press. Much other work is done besides this.

It would be interesting to know whether such chaotic conditions are more effective in producing saints than the methods of the West. Here everyone has to struggle for himself, even against his fellow disciples. He has to run far to find a quiet place for meditation and studies, unless he is so advanced that he can shut himself away from all the noises around him. He must also overcome all ideas of *sattvic* (pure) food, or any type of special diet so beautifully described in yoga books. He must develop immunity against insects and vermin of all kinds — bedbugs, mosquitoes, flies, mice, rats. He must be able to drink water from the Ganges without shivering at the things floating in his cup and eat from dishes that have been "washed" by dipping in the cold Ganges without soap, and without even being wiped off.

In a Catholic monastery conditions are austere, but the monk or nun will sleep in a proper bed in a spotlessly clean room with proper sanitary facilities. In the West we take for granted such comforts, considering them bare necessities, but in India they are found only in luxury hotels, seldom in private houses. No wonder we Westerners are a constant headache to the swamis who are responsible for our welfare!

I missed meditation again this morning because of the bedbugs. Nearly every square inch of my body is bitten and swollen. Lila advises me that I must collect the bugs in paper and throw them out. "No killing," she says, "Swami Sivananda does not permit any killing." I refrained from mentioning her contradictory statements made just recently. I have put the legs of my bed in tin cans filled with water as protection from the bugs, as they cannot crawl over water. But bedbugs crawl up the walls, then across the ceiling and drop on the bed from above. The tins of water protect against worms, ants and spiders, but the bedbugs are too clever. Although it is disgusting for the victim, one cannot help but admire their intelligence.

27 September

The Eastern mind is certainly different

from the Western one. For the last few days, Gurudev would address somebody in the group and say, pointing to me, "Have you met this lady from Kashmir?" or "Come over here and meet my friend from Kashmir." That seems to me rather silly. I can't see the point in such a remark. Maybe I don't have a sense of humor, or at least not the Eastern type of humor. Is there something wrong with me? Yesterday Mrs. Radner came with her two boys to visit her husband. I happened to meet them and Gurudev in time to hear the younger boy, about 8 years old, look up at the towering figure of Sivananda and say, "I have heard you are a great yogi. People say yogis have powers, but I don't believe it."

I looked at Master's face to see his reaction, but he just smiled and said, "What must I do to prove that I am a yogi?"

The little boy was taken aback. He tried quickly to think of some request to make and after a moment said, "Let's go to the river and you get all the little fishes to come to you. And then all the big fishes."

Master obligingly turned and went to the Ganges. The two boys followed and, of course, I did too, being as curious as they were. We all stared at Master, who had his eyes closed as if he were deep in thought. Then he bent down, put his right hand into the water, moved it back and forth and murmured something, which I suspect was a kind of mantra. In watching him, we almost missed the arrival of the fishes, which were by now swimming in great numbers around his hand. The little boy was jumping up and down, very excited, and even his brother, who was 14, was obviously very impressed. I was stunned. The little boy in his excitement cried, "Now the big fishes!"

Master turned to him and said, "No, that would not be right. First we have to wait until the little fishes go home. If we call the big ones while they are still here, we would trap the little fishes."

Master said we would have to be absolutely quiet for a few minutes, so we sat there waiting as the small fishes dispersed. After some time, which seemed to be endless for the little boy, but was probably only 5 or 6 minutes, all the fishes had left. Gurudev put his left hand into the water and murmured something. I wondered if it were a different mantra for the big ones.

I thought, "What would happen if I stepped into the water? Would the fish take off as they do at other times?" Resisting the temptation only for a moment, I found myself in the water up to my knees. The big fishes came, swam around my legs, nipping the oxygen bubbles. I remembered some chapati in my bag and made tiny little balls of it, lowering them into the water. The fish took them from my hand. Their eyes turned toward me — were they looking at me? What a surprise — fish have faces! They have very individual faces and expressions! I wondered if I could pet them and I started to caress them with the tips of my fingers. What a thrilling experience! I had never before in my life caressed fish. I had never heard of anybody doing this. I felt elated.

Gurudev sat on the steps, became quiet and said, "We should let the fish go home now. It is getting late for them."

The little boy said with great conviction, looking up into his eyes, "Now I know you are a great yogi, and I will tell everybody."

After Master retired to his kutir, the two children ran to the main section of the ashram and told of their recent experience at the tops of their voices. Everybody was impressed, and I, as the only adult witness, was questioned in detail. Could it have been an accident? Do the fish come at certain times to eat? Did Gurudev throw food into the water? I gave my side of the experience and by so doing stirred up my own thoughts. I have heard the expression, "Lord Krishna and his lila." Lila means games. The Lord plays the lila, the divine comedy. Was Gurudev playing a divine comedy or lila? To what purpose? What did he have in mind? And why did he call me the lady from Kashmir? Is there more to that than I understand?

28 September

Last night I decided to sit on the stone stairs during satsang instead of on a chair because I think it is from the chairs that I get the bedbugs. Master called me over to him. "Why don't you sit on the chair?" he asked. I said nothing, but obeyed. He added, "I got it especially for you."

After a long pause, Swami Vishnudevananda, seeing my embarrassment, answered for me, "Swamiji, she does not like bedbugs and she thinks she picks them up from the chair."

"Is that so?" Master asked.

I admitted it and said, "I cannot see what bugs and dirt have to do with religion."

"Ha, you cannot see what bugs have to do with religion?" He seemed quite astonished.

"Chidanandaji," he called another swami who, I suspect, is someday to be Master's successor, "Chidanandaji, tell Mrs. Hellman the story of the devotee of Lord Krishna."

Swamiji took me a little away from the scene so that we would not disturb the kirtan with our talk. "You are having trouble with bugs, Mother?" he laughed. "Yes, I understand. It must be very difficult for you to live here. I will tell you the story the Master asked me to narrate.

"There was a devotee who meditated intensely on Lord Krishna. He was so much absorbed that he forgot to eat, drink and to look after his physical needs. His body became so much neglected that lice settled on it. While he was in deep meditation he was not even aware of them. But finally when the lice multiplied more and more, he felt disturbed in his meditation on the Lord. So he began to pray: 'Oh Lord Krishna, my mind wants constantly to dwell on You only, but now these lice are disturbing my concentration on You. Please free me from these lice.'

"Because the Lord was so pleased with His devotee, He granted him a vision. He embraced him and took all the lice away onto His own body. The devotee was deeply shocked. 'Oh no, Lord, I did not mean that You should trouble Yourself. Please give them all back to me, but grant me one thing: give me the strength that my mind will go above the lice and so constantly dwell on Thee.' At once the devotee got Liberation.

"Think about it," Swami Chidananda laughed again, although he showed sympathy for my troubles. "Everything will come in time." There was silence between us. Swamiji's face became very

Sivananda with Swami Chidananda and the author. "He must be one of the most devoted disciples of the Master."

transparent — I would not have thought that such transparency could occur in a brown skin. He must be one of the most devoted disciples of the Master.

"Mother," he said, making his *pranam*, "may I take leave of you? Some other time I will tell you about Lord Siva and the Law of Karma." I felt embarrassed at his bow. Humility, true humility. What a wonderful soul!

29 *September*

Swami Venkatesananda

is correctly described as Swami Bliss not only because of the smile in his eyes, but also his naturalness and sense of humor, his kindness and helpfulness. He seems to have a sixth sense, knowing when thoughts of confusion cloud my mind. I heard the sound of the veena playing inside his kutir but I did not want to be a pest and disturb him at all hours. Suddenly he appeared in the doorway and said, "What is troubling you?"

I told him of my grave thoughts about the Law of Karma, of Chidananadji's story of Lord Krishna and the lice and that I wondered what the story of Siva and the Law of Karma would be. Venkatesanandaji immediately offered to tell me the story in the hope that it would ease my worries.

"It must have been about the same hour of the day as this," he began, "when a peasant woman was waiting for her husband to come home from the fields. It was already later than he usually came and when she looked up she saw the body of her husband pierced on the dead branch of a tree. She lamented loudly and, with no one to help her, had great difficulty in getting his body down and laying him on the ground. Then she complained to Lord Siva, 'You are supposed to be the Compassionate Lord. Every day we worship Thee. This was a good husband and a good father to my children. Why have you done this to me and to him?'

"Because of her sincerity, Lord Siva granted her a vision and said, 'If one has killed, one will also be killed.' To this the woman replied, 'I don't know of anybody he has killed. How can you make such a statement?' Then Lord Siva told her that the husband had once pierced a needle through a bug."

At this point I became so upset that I wanted to run away, but Swamiji helped me by saying, "No, no, no. Wait, hear the end of the story. The woman said to the Lord, 'How old was he?' to which Lord Siva replied, 'Twelve years.' 'But, Lord,' she cried, 'You must know that little boys of twelve have no common sense, cannot assess the consequences of their actions. How can You be so cruel?'

"Then Lord Siva had to really prove himself as the Compassionate Lord and suggested to her that she put some ashes from the morning worship on her husband's wound, and his life would be restored."

However, my distress only increased. I objected violently, "But who can know all one's wrong actions in life? And what about all the ones from past lives? There is simply no hope."

Suddenly Venkatesanandaji's face grew very serious and all the mischievousness and joking disappeared from his voice. Looking at me almost as intently as Gurudev he said, "This law applies only as long as you think you are the doer." At this moment a wave of gratitude overcame me for this glimmer of hope. I bowed to him and left for my favorite rock on the Ganges to reflect on this.

Today Lila told me that

tomorrow a small party is going to Vasistha Guha where I would meet Swami Purushatthamananda, the saint who blesses by beating his devotee on the back. She urged me to come along.

* * * * *

Tonight I looked up at the black sky with the stars shining with a brightness I had never seen before. Some great law does govern this multitude of stars, planets, suns. It seems logical that the same law governs everything, right down to the tiniest speck of dust. What a terrible thought! That means that there is nothing so small that it can escape that law. It seems utterly hopeless. Yet there is the other side to the Divine Law—the Law of Reincarnation—another chance. One can see the working of this law all around us, in all things—strange that we never take the trouble to really become aware of it. The few who do are the saints, the Self-realized persons to whom we look for guidance. I wonder if Swami Sivananda is guiding my thoughts right now. Is he far from me? Am I far from him? Is all that I have experienced nothing but a fancy of my own mind? What kind of law makes me think like this?

There above is the beautiful night sky, millions of worlds. Here am I, this little speck of dust, so small it cannot even be measured in comparison to that unimaginable vastness, yet is a part of it. Perhaps assuming myself to be so unimportant is just another kind of vanity.

1 October

This morning the Master refused a gift, suggesting very nicely how the person should make use of it herself. After she left, I asked him about refusing gifts. He said, "A present must be given with a pure heart, with the real spirit of giving. If the giver will regret it, then it is better not to accept it. Also a gift should be refused if the giver is trying to buy his way to the teacher."

After lunch Lila came rushing into my kutir to say we would leave in 5 minutes to go to Vasistha Guha. "Think of some questions to ask Swami Purushatthamananda," she said. There were four of us in the party and the bus drove along the serpentine curves of the Ganges. It was very beautiful, a wild kind of beauty. As the road became more precipitous, I became quite frightened. Looking down through the window I could not see one inch of road, only rocks, and our driver kept turning around in his seat and talking to someone in the bus. It seemed to me it would take the most skillful driver, paying close attention, to keep the vehicle on the road. This man hardly had his eyes on the road at all. However, somehow the dangerous ride did come safely to an end. We got out and climbed down the rocks. Lila, who knew the way, led us down a narrow trail. At last we came to an open space that looked as though it had been dipped in gold.

Suddenly we saw the saint, his robe a vibrant orange. His snow-white hair and beard glistened in the sun. It was like something out of a dream, unreal.

Sylvia Hellman, Swami Sivananda and Swami Purushatthamananda. "As I gave my *pranam* to the saint, silently I gave him the name 'Dear God in Heaven.' "

As I gave my *pranam* to the saint, silently I gave him a name "Dear God in Heaven." He was so perfectly the picture of God I had as a child. He led us to his cave while Lila told him about the visitors she had brought. He took his seat on a stone bench in front of his cave and offered us the opposite bench. Some sat here, some on the ground.

Two of the visitors wanted their picture taken with him. Instead of replying, he got up and motioned us to a little straw hut covered with branches and leaves to protect him from the sun while meditating. He showed me the place where he wanted me to sit down and then, before I realized what was happening, he dropped himself into my lap! He was very light, but nevertheless it was so unexpected that I had to tense my muscles to keep my balance and hold him steady. When asked what he was doing, he replied with great simplicity. "I am her little child. I am sitting in Divine Mother's lap." While pictures were being taken with some of the others, I thought about this incident. He apparently can see the Divine in everything. My self-criticism and my awareness of my shortcomings prevent me from recognizing my own divinity.

Swamiji told us that his cave had originally been discovered by a great saint, Vasistha, which is why it is known as Vasistha Guha (guha means cave). After that, for a long time the cave was a lion's den, until Swamiji rediscovered it and took possession. He carried up stones from the Ganges to close off part of what must at some time have been an underground stream. It is several miles long and about five feet high. I peered with a flashlight over the stone wall he had erected halfway up and I could not see the end.

I was impressed with how great his faith must have been when he first occupied the cave, considering that the mountain lions of the region could easily have come during the night. He did not have matches and he had very little food, but members of the surrounding hill tribes, after seeing him fetching water from the Ganges, brought him matches and grain and milk. Moved by their kindness, Swamiji offered to teach their children, so he has continued to live in the cave for more than 30 years. He has no disciples but he does allow people to stay with him for a year. Being with him gave me a wonderful sense of peace and tranquility. I was glad I had come.

He told me I could see the cave and one of his pupils brought a flashlight to show me the way. I saw his seat for meditation, which was a wooden board, and in a little niche that served as a shrine the Sivalinga was installed. The walls were just the natural rock of the cave. When I came out and thanked him, he said, "You can stay for some time and meditate if you like." I was only too happy to accept and went back into the cave.

After a period of struggle, I was finally able to calm my wild mind. How many minutes of stillness passed I do not know, but suddenly I heard some beautiful sounds, like the singing of little birds, lovely and sweet.

When I came out of the cave, the saint said, "Now she has a nice smile on her face. She must have had a nice experience."

"Yes," I answered, "you know it? There was lovely sweet singing, as from little birds. But when I opened my eyes and they became accustomed to the darkness, I could not discover the nests. What was it?"

He chuckled. "You don't understand anything yet. Did it ever occur to you that rocks also have voices?"

Then he asked me, "What do you want me to do for you?"

Lila nudged me and whispered, "Ask him about your guru."

I felt such a question in front of others would be most unfair to Sivananda, who had been so kind to me. Swami Purushatthamananda asked me again so I finally said, "What is the purpose of my coming to India?"

His answer showed me what insight and understanding of people he had. He said simply, "Purify your mind." He recognized my conflicts. He could see where the trouble lay.

I did not discover the full meaning of his words immediately. At first I thought with resignation, "All right, I know I am not perfect, otherwise I would not be struggling, but would already be a master, not an aspirant, on the spiritual path." But later I realized that he had given a direct answer to the question in my mind. It was as if he were sitting by my side and whispering in my ear, "Only Sivananda himself can answer the question that is pressing your heart." Of course! How simple! Why not go to the one who could give the answer? I hope there will be an opportunity to ask Gurudev without witnesses. The faith of others must not be disturbed.

I looked about me. Over the entrance to the cave were pictures of Sri Ramakrishna, Sarada Devi, his wife, and Swami Vivekananda, Ramakrishna's chief disciple, together with some other pictures of divine incarnations. One of his pupils told me, "He is a disciple of Swami Brahmananda, the spiritual son of Sri Ramakrishna."

Swami Purushatthamananda introduced me to a German lady who is a guest in one of his caves. She is tall, middle-aged, a former actress, dressed in Indian fashion and has spent the last six years in India, mainly with the Ramakrishna Mission. We talked for a little while and she urged me to go down to Madras to meet Swami Krishnaprem, whom she described as an exceptional person among the sannyasins. Then she asked me if I could get her some cigarettes in Rishikesh and send them with other visitors.

I was amazed. I could not put the two things together. Here she could live fearlessly in a cave all by herself, sleep on rocks without proper covering, go without proper food, walk barefoot and live without all the other things that women think so important, yet she was addicted to smoking. Strange. It makes me wonder how important this renunciation really is, except for the practice of discipline.

Before we left, I tried to put a ten-rupee note among some of Swamiji's papers while he was sitting with his eyes closed. But he was aware of what I had done and took the money and placed it back in my hand. I was deeply shocked and hurt. Was I the type of person Master had spoken about from whom gifts should not be accepted because they might later regret the gift? I was sure I was not. Why then did he refuse to accept my little gift? Oh, these saints! Sometimes it is difficult to see the saintliness. Swamiji saw my confusion. "You keep that money," he said gently. "You don't have enough yourself. Someday when you have plenty you can give some to me." He laughed his giggling laugh, and I understood.

As we were waiting for the bus he came over to me. "Learn as much as you can," he said, "You will need it when you return to the West. It will be good for you to be well prepared to meet the people."

"But I will stay here," I said. "I brought all my things with me to stay here. And Swami Sivananda wrote to me that I would be coming home." I surprised myself with such a definite statement.

"But you will not stay here," he answered. "You will have to go back and become a teacher in the West."

At that moment the bus arrived. Lila sat down beside me. "You see?" she said. "You will become a teacher in the West. You should. . ." I interrupted her with a burst of laughter. What do these people know about me? On what is their opinion grounded? One does not become a saint in a few months. A miracle would have to happen. At present I am as dark in my heart as I have ever been.

The bus began to sway so badly that many people became ill. From early childhood I have suffered from motion sickness. The bus was crowded with farmers, laborers in torn clothes, dirty and smelly, who frequently indulged in the unpleasant habit of spitting. I was filled with disgust and my stomach started to heave. A cramp began to develop. But I have read that everything takes place in the mind. If I don't allow my mind to accept a sick stomach, I cannot be sick. I forced my mind to turn back to "Dear God in Heaven" and dwelt on my experience at his cave for the rest of the journey. For almost the first time in my life I did not get sick in a moving vehicle.

2 October

This morning Sivananda asked me,

"You have been to Vasistha Guha?"

"Yes, I have."

"How did you like it?"

"It was like paradise!" I answered reproachfully. He remained kind and smiling. Later he gave me some fruit, but there was something in his look that irritated me. After satsang he went as usual to his kutir in the company of some visitors and the swamis they call his bodyguards.

Suddenly he turned to me. "You like cocoa?"

"Yes," I answered grimly, wondering what the cocoa had to do with anything. I have not come for cocoa—I can drink it much more comfortably, and more cheaply, in Canada—but I followed him into his kitchen. He moved two chairs close together, took his seat in one and offered me the second. The others dispersed, knowing the Master wanted to speak to me privately.

"You are very restless," he said, while the cook, who spoke no English, was making the cocoa. "Why?"

That was too much for me. I burst out, "You should know!" and silently I added, "*If* you are a guru."

Master remained silent as the tension became almost unbearable. Finally he spoke, "You are very restless. It is time to clear your doubts."

There it was, the word that had been haunting me all these days. In that instant all doubts were gone and an indescribable feeling of peace flowed through my whole body. He continued, "You have been very close to me in previous births. Now you have come again." He paused and I waited, scarcely daring to breathe, lest I disturb this precious flow of thought. Then he said, "I will reveal to you everything, but you must have patience. Wait."

Another long pause, and then, reproachfully, "You kept me waiting a long time. But now you are here."

"But Gurudev," I nearly sobbed, "why didn't you call me earlier?"

"You were so ambitious."

The cook brought the cocoa. I decided to ask a question that had been bothering me. "Gurudev, is it really true that you showed me this ashram long ago, when I was only in my teens? I recognized it at once, but many parts have been built within the last few years and I am now 44. How can this be?"

He answered simply, "There is no space, no time. There is little difference, seen from a distance, between the ashram you see now and the view you saw. Your vision was a projection into the future, but really there is no space, no time." After he had finished his cocoa he repeated, "You have kept me waiting for a long time, but now you are here." With that he got up and left the kitchen.

I did not feel like returning to my kutir so I went down and sat on one of the huge rocks in the Ganges. I had much to think about. Sivananda. Siva-ananda. Lord Siva, the God of destruction of all obstacles. Ananda—bliss. Siva is bliss. Ayyapan told me that according to Hindu belief, Lord Siva is the Compassionate One, the most easy to please. He drank the poison of the world, that is why his throat is blue and he is called Nilankanta. Lord Siva is supposed to be the most forgiving one. Swami Sivananda is the most forgiving friend.

This day I have experienced his understanding. From the sound of my voice, from the expression on my face, he must have known what I was feeling and thinking—my irritation, my impatience, my doubts. Yet he gave me the reassurance I needed.

3 October

This morning a new visitor arrived who turned out to be a wonderful musician. His name is Gopalakrishna Dikshitar. He placed his porcelain bowls in a semi-circle around him, carefully arranged by size, and then proceeded to pour water back and forth in very small quantities, "tuning his bowls," almost like a pharmacist mixing the ingredients of a medicine. The scene was like a picture. The Ganges shone blue and green in the sun with millions of little sparkles. Gopalakrishna's black hair and brown body, with the red marks on his forehead, stood out in front of the whitewashed building of the Diamond Jubilee Hall, whose doors added a dark green. A swami came with the harmonium, his orange robe giving another colorful touch. Gopalakrishna began to play on his bowls with light sticks and the beautiful sweet sound of his water bowl music, called Jalataranagan, filled the air.

Someone notified the Master and a seat was prepared for him, as more and more people gathered around. I had my eyes fixed on Sivananda and I saw his eyes begin to sparkle. Suddenly he got up and sat next to Gopalakrishna, who offered him his sticks and Sivananda played a melody of his own, adding the same cascades he had heard the musician play. We all laughed joyfully. It was one of those rare moments when Sivananda seemed to be one of us, sharing with us the same feelings of joy. Then he called me over. "You should record this and take it back to America." Gopalakrishna agreed to perform again between 3 and 4 o'clock in the afternoon .

When the time came, several other swamis volunteered to play drums in accompaniment. They seemed to know what was being played, without a word being exchanged. A professor of music, Mr. Shastri, explained to me that one sound of the strings tells the musician which raga or ragini is being played. Every musician knows between 300 and 400 ragas, so when Gopalakrishna gives the signal, the others know which one he is going to play.

4 *October*

Many visitors are still coming,

others have returned to their homes. Whenever Sivananda is outside his kutir I am right beside him, listening to what he says, what advice he gives, watching how he treats people. The most critical mind cannot deny he has outstanding qualities. Never is anyone kept waiting because Sivananda wants to play the big boss or wants the visitor to feel humble before him. Even some of his disciples interrupt him when he is in conversation with a guest, yet he never scolds them in front of others for such conduct. Western visitors often demand that he exhibit his supernatural powers to prove his mastership. He just smiles at them, gives them sweets, fruits, spiritual gifts, knowing they are like children.

"Live a good spiritual life," he encourages them, "and all powers will come to you too." He does not yield to the temptation to convince them of his greatness. What does it matter whether anyone can see a great yogi in him or not?

Swami Sivananda playing the *jalataranagar* (water bowls). With arms crossed, Gopalakrishna Dikshitar watches and smiles.

With no regular income, the existence of the ashram with hospital, pharmacy, printing shop, book department, magazine section, 200 permanent residents and an average of a hundred visitors — is that not a miracle? *Sadhus,* pilgrims of all nationalities are given shelter, food and medical treatment at no charge. Thousands of books are given away free, and the postage costs thousands of rupees a year. A primary school is maintained where the children are fed, clothed and educated. The leper colony, now a settlement in itself, is still assisted with clothing, blankets and other necessities. Somehow the money that is needed flows into the ashram.

Now that I have had Gurudev's assurance that he will clear all my doubts if I show patience, life in the ashram has become a paradise. I laugh with everyone, joke with everyone. I take advice, instructions, spiritual help from everyone who has something to give.

At satsang Master loves to give presents, usually fruits and sweets. Tonight he was also giving saris. For me he chose a mauve one. My surprise amused him. Tomorrow I will have to go to the bazaar to buy material for a slip and a blouse. Sivananda gives all these presents to implant in the disciples a certainty that he cares for them. Eventually no visible sign is necessary, when the disciple has grown to the stage where he or she is fully aware of that love.

5 October

Someone has decided that my cottage

is too far from the main buildings of the ashram, since there are apparently unsavoury characters roaming around Rishikesh and Hardwar, and that I must move to another kutir. Swami Paramananda and I went to the new place which he has made very attractive. He said, "Here you have all day and night the view of your guru's kutir, as well as the holy Ganges. I will see that you get a small electric stove so that you may have your tea whenever you like and can also heat your food. Here you can write your letters and see the Master coming from his kutir. You will need a table lamp for writing at night. I shall see to your comfort personally." Swamiji is not only a good diplomat, but also has a charming way of having things done his way. All my luggage was moved and I am now in the very center of the ashram.

I went outside to wait until I saw Gurudev leaving for his office and was standing near the kutir of Swami Venkatesananda. He greeted me with a happy smile. "Waiting for Gurudev? Come in here!" He offered me a seat in his room and showed me his veena, which is a masterpiece of Indian artistry, inlaid with ivory and colorfully painted. Then he handed me a booklet. "Have a look at this. It may answer some questions for you." It did indeed. A chart gave the location of the chakras (also called lotuses) relating them to the veena, his instrument, showing where the locations of certain notes or sounds are equivalent to the lotuses. "You can copy that," he said, handing me a paper and pencil, which I proceeded to do.

Then I joined the people who were following the Master to his office. He stopped and turned to me, pointing to the top of a flight of wide steps high up on the banks of the Ganges where a horrifying figure was standing. "Go and meet your friend," he said. "Oh no, Gurudev! He hardly looks like a human being!" Gently Master corrected me. "You must learn to understand. He

"The sadhu says he has come to give you his *pranam*
and to return your property."

looks like that because he follows the old tradition. He has covered his body with ashes to remind himself that the body is nothing. The ashes also have the effect of keeping him cool in summer and warm in winter. He is a holy man. Go and meet him. Give him some milk, tea, whatever he likes."

The *sadhu* was now coming down the steps and I rather uneasily approached him and gave him my *pranam*. He had a bundle of cloth, knotted together, which he put down in order to give me his *pranam* and a bow. I was surprised but when I looked into his wonderful eyes, I felt comfortable. From his bundle he took out two oranges and two bananas and, with an indescribable smile, handed them to me.

I turned to Gurudev and asked, "Gurudev, what am I going to do? He is giving me fruit. Is it not customary that I should give him fruit?"

Master had a mischievous smile on his face. "Take him to your kutir and give him something, tea and biscuits." (Master had spoken to me in English and the *sadhu* spoke only Hindi.)

The *sadhu* followed me to my kutir where I offered him a seat. By gestures I tried to find out what he would like to eat or drink. He refused everything except an orange, which he peeled at once and shared half with me. He was a strange sight sitting there, almost naked, wearing a loin cloth that was so tiny it could not have been smaller if it were to serve any purpose at all. On his head he had a mass of matted hair, more reddish than black in color, which was wound round like a woman's bun. The ashes gave his brown skin a bluish tint; the sacred marks on his forehead were greyish white.

He brought out of his bundle a container, a dried gourd, and indicated that I should take it. I saw there were some coins in it and I thought he wanted me to put some money in, but he shook his head. I couldn't understand what he wanted so I went to the swami next door for some help. He explained, "The *sadhu* says he has come to give you his *pranam* and to return your property."

I realized that the gourd was a begging bowl. I took out the coins, which were dated in the 1940s, and I said to Swamiji that I have only just come to India so it could not be my property.

Swamiji and the *sadhu* had some conversation in Hindi and then Swamiji said, "He insists this is your property. The amount of money is correct, even if they are not the same coins." Swamiji went back to his kutir.

I looked at the *sadhu*. His eyes assumed a faraway look, then he half-closed them. I entered into the silence. I have no idea how much time passed—it seemed endless, yet short. What is time, after all? The *sadhu* opened his eyes and, with the same sweet smile, he *pranamed* again and left the room. This peaceful mood remained with me.

6 October

A certain routine has developed.

Each day hatha yoga classes are held at 6 a.m. in the Bhajan Hall. There are about 20 of us, taught by Swami Vishnudevananda, who gives excellent instruction in different yoga postures and pranayama. He came to the ashram when he was 18 (he is now about 25) and made the decision to strive for a higher life as a disciple of Sivananda. Gurudev knows how to implant high ideals in the young, how to stir up their thinking and inspire them to follow the spiritual path. He provides food, clothing and shelter for them so that their minds can be free from worry about the needs of everyday life and they can devote their time to spiritual practice.

Few can spend many hours in prayer, meditation, study of scriptures and hatha yoga, and so to keep their young minds from wasting precious time in idle gossip or laziness, he utilizes their strength and abilities for the good of others. Selfless service brings purification, and who is not in need of this? When we invite a friend to our home, we see that our house is clean and comfortable. How much more should we clean out our minds when we invite God to come in?

We also have classes in raja yoga, Vedanta and the Gita. The Master teaches that there should always be a healthy combination of yogas for harmonious spiritual growth. He has composed a little song to make this understandable for the student:

Eat a little
Drink a little
Sleep a little
Pray a little
Do Japa a little
Work a little
Meditate a little.

The ashram is a happy place. There is really no western equivalent for an ashram in India. Ashram means "dwelling quarters of a spiritual teacher"—a saint, who gives shelter to students who wish to be trained by him and whom he is willing to accept. No fees are asked by the teacher, but it is an unwritten law that the students in turn take care of their teacher's physical needs. The student does this in two ways: by making a financial contribution and giving service. From the number of buildings in the ashram, one can see that Swami Sivananda has had many devoted students.

As Swami Chidananda, who teaches the raja yoga classes, explained, the classes are set up to give Westerners something they can take home. Actually, study with a Master is not a question of classes, but of practice, every minute of the day—hatha yoga, pranayama, reading the scriptures or the Master's teachings, and reflection. The Master makes himself always available to us. The student is expected to reflect on the findings of periods of introspection and to analyze them. At a given time the results are laid before the guru, weaknesses and mistakes are admitted, and help and advice are requested. "I can tell you," Swamiji said, "Gurudev takes more interest in the spiritual diaries of his students than in anything else."

Before satsang this evening

I took my place on the steps by the Ganges in front of Master's door. He saw me and called me into the veranda, where I was brought some tea. Then he said, "Why did you come?" He pointed to the bench on which he was sitting. "Sit here." When I hesitated, he added, "You were very close to me in a previous birth. Sit here now." After a little pause he said, "You were bound to come." He was all tenderness, love and kindness.

I was extremely happy and full of hope as together we went to satsang. I feel that soon he will answer my question: Is he my guru?

At satsang I was sitting in a chair near Gurudev when a cow came over and sniffed me. Before I knew what was happening, she had relieved herself, letting nature have free run all over me. Everybody laughed and Master said, "Now you are christened."

I joined in the laughter." A very unusual way of christening people!" Later I marvelled that I had not been embarrassed. Was that because cows are considered sacred here?

Another Western visitor,

Mr. Orland, arrived today. He made great efforts to convince us all that he was very advanced. He had read everything, understood everything, and had come to the ashram not to learn but only for the special blessing of Sri Gurudev. The handsome swami whom Lila calls "the young centurion," gave the visitor the usual living quarters near the Ganges, but when he heard that there were some more secluded kutirs in the forest he protested that he was very advanced and would be most happy to have the seclusion and quietness of one of these. He let it be known that he would come to satsang tomorrow. Being very tired, he preferred to settle in his new quarters and go to bed early.

Shortly after ten o'clock tonight we were amazed to see a figure come leaping down the steps and onto the roof where we were gathered for satsang. He was wearing pyjamas, the top flying open in his great excitement. What happened? This new, very advanced visitor tried to tell Master something. His words cascaded, his arms and hands gesticulating wildly.

The young centurion swami explained what had happened. Mr. Orland had been lying down on his cot with a blanket and was just falling asleep when he became aware of a weight on his body. It was becoming heavier and heavier and moving up towards his chest. Suddenly he was fully awake and found himself facing a 16 foot coiled-up snake! Swamiji thinks it was a python.

Gurudev looked at Swami Atmananda, who assured him that he had checked the holes where the walls met the floors and they were both open. At this Mr. Orland interjected, "Yes, yes. I closed them up."

"But the snake never leaves through the same hole by which it enters," Gurudev explained. "There would have been no problem had you left those holes open." He turned to Swamiji, "Get him a room on the compound." This time Mr. Orland did not object.

Since satsang had been disrupted by this incident, I decided that it was time for me to leave and go to bed. I met Swamiji outside carrying out Master's wishes. He lived in one of the little huts in the forest and had a big flashlight which he would swing to keep the wild animals at a respectful distance. He was feeling very annoyed at Mr. Orland, and he took out his frustration on one of the stray dogs, hitting it with the heavy flashlight. The poor animal yelped. It was covered with sores and bloody boils from malnutrition. I could not help saying, "In Canada such brutality is interpreted as suppressed sex. Maybe instead of being a swami you had better get married." I realized that being so outspoken would make me more enemies than friends and that I was really just venting my disappointment that a swami should fall so far short of being a "god on earth." Even if somebody is a god still in the making, according to my views he must not vent his anger on a helpless creature. A few days ago I saw a cow die of starvation, its body swollen from the heat. To my mind it would have been better and kinder to kill it. The so-called virtue of non-killing, of eating no meat, can hardly justify such brutality or indifference.

10 October

It is three o'clock in the morning.

I have just awakened, clear-headed and wonderfully rested. It is not yet dawn and the moon and stars stand out brilliantly against the black velvet of the sky. A cool little wind has come up, like a gentle caress. The quietness makes it possible to become aware of subtle sounds. I can hear the beat of my heart. I'm sitting in the old deckchair Swami Paramananda brought for me where I can relax physically and forget the body. The thoughts are beginning to flow.

Swami Sivananda is often reluctant to answer and quick to brush aside things that to him, the great one, are unimportant. But they are not unimportant to the little beginner who has come from a totally different background. His jokes and stories do help to break down the barrier the novice feels between herself and the Master. They create an atmosphere of closeness, which is necessary to serve as the first stepping stone.

How wonderful it is when one can gather all the rays of spiritual love and tenderness from his voice, undisturbed by the loud voices of other people, when one can read unspoken words of understanding in his eyes. On the spiritual path it seems that the struggles and suffering are tremendous in proportion to the success. Motherly and fatherly guidance is needed from one who knows all about the tribulations that have to be faced. In ordinary life, the world, especially the business world, is very impersonal. Even within a family one can be left with feelings of loneliness, longing for love and acceptance. On the spiritual path this loneliness does not seem to diminish.

Slowly I begin to have more of a grasp of Sivananda's wisdom. All Gurudev's gifts and attention are meant to implant in students feelings of affection, of being wanted as his devotee. It often appears that the weaker the student, the more attention is given, since each receives exactly what is needed. From some he demands a great deal, sometimes the seemingly impossible. This is determined individually by what he senses in each devotee. I have noticed that occasionally he will speak directly, at other times just hint. It has also happened that he will give the answer before the question is asked.

There is a craving in every individual, no matter how unaware, to experience other states of consciousness, to understand the truth about God, the cosmos, the universe. In some people this craving finds no rest. It becomes the driving force, unequalled in other areas, to pursue the spiritual path.

Sitting with Swami Sivananda by the River Ganges.
"Sit here, it is all right. You have been very close to me before."

11 October

The office was crowded this morning.

There was a young mother with her baby whom she was trying to keep quiet so that he would not disturb the great guru. When she made a move to leave, Sivananda brushed her worry aside and said, "You can stay here. It is all music to me." It was not music to me — and I have a long way to go before I will be able to say that it is!

After lunch Swami Paramananda came to inform me that the Master was willing to pose for pictures wearing the cross I gave him. I knew the people at home would enjoy having such a picture. He chose a big boulder by the Ganges to sit on and I was supposed to sit beside him. But the side of the stone was slanting so I did not dare to sit down, as there was no room for a respectful distance. He waved my hesitation away. "Sit here, it is all right. You have been very close to me before."

Tonight he surprised me by telling everybody, "She is my auntie." What did he mean? My mind began to imagine the wildest reasons for his remark. Did he want to see if I would become disrespectful? Was the joke meant for somebody else? Whatever he had in mind, I have decided to respond, if he should repeat it. One is never really sure in dealing with a saint. I just have to remember the old saint in the cave to see how peculiarly they can behave.

12 October

A Western teenager asked me to

teach her a few movements of Indian dancing. As I was showing her one of the mudras, which requires moving the fingers into intricate positions, she suddenly lost her self-control and slapped me on the hand. My first reaction was surprise, then, as I became aware that a great number of people had gathered to watch, I became angry and without saying anything left the scene. Two hours later in the Master's office, he said, for no apparent reason, "Anger remains, expands through its waves and is injurious to everybody and to one's own self. Overcome anger." How did he know? Maybe somebody told him.

Later in the day, when I had an opportunity to see him alone, I approached him to confess the incident. "Anger lingers for a long time," he explained, and handed me a little booklet, *How to Conquer Anger.* He continued, "One moment of anger destroys many good thoughts. Even if we have forgotten, unknowingly anger sends out its waves."

I was very touched at how gently Master tried to teach me. He shows so much concern for my spiritual development without a trace of authoritative power, like a loving father. My intuition has proved to be right in guiding me to hand myself over to him. I would have liked very much at that moment to bow to him, as the Indians do, so grateful do I feel for his concern, but my pride does not allow me such a gesture.

The most precious moments for me are those when I am permitted to be alone with him in his kutir, or at least without the distraction of a group of other people, talking at the tops of their voices. Since I find his accent hard to understand, it requires great concentration for me to hear all that the Master says, and I become tired and irritated with the chatter going on when he is speaking. But these nights in his kutir allow me to come to an inner stillness, an awareness of the sacredness of such moments.

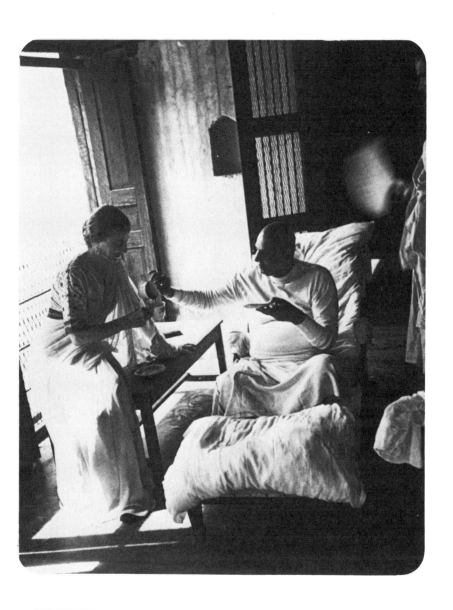

Gurudev's gesture of sharing his coffee is symbolic of sharing his spiritual wealth. This brings a smile to Swami Satchitananda who is fanning Master's face.

Gurudev distributing *prasad* (sweets) to the children at the ashram.

A change takes place in the Master himself. Sometimes his eyes reflect an indescribable love, a love not from this world. I hesitate to limit it to words, which may give rise to wrong thoughts, false sentiments.

Tonight I did not expect another invitation to his kutir, but Gurudev calls and helps when one needs it most. He handed me a beautifully embroidered Kashmir shawl, as well as a marble stone engraved with the Sanskrit letter *Om*, the symbolic sign of God, a garland of flowers and some fruit. Then I realized he is ever ready to reward the disciple who willingly confesses or admits weaknesses, and as long as the invisible reward cannot be seen by the aspirant, Sivananda expresses it through gifts.

13 October

There is a little boy who comes from the Master's kitchen with milk, butter, biscuits and fruit for me. Gurudev calls him Sunnyboy, he is so happy and bright. But in his few words of English today he managed to tell me that he suffers from headaches. He cuddled close to me, putting his head in my lap. Any woman would understand what the real trouble is — lack of love and affection. He is in the company of men only, men concerned with their own spiritual development.

Sunnyboy is one of a number of orphans who are taken care of at the ashram, given free schooling, shelter, food, clothes and candies or Indian sweets from the Master. If they are promising, industrious students, he will even send them to university or college, paying all the cost or helping them to get scholarships. High ideals are implanted in these orphan boys, but there is no expectation or pressure on them to become *sannyasins*. The Master believes in inner freedom. But if he becomes aware of strong spiritual tendencies, he will encourage and strengthen them.

The weather in October here is as hot as midsummer in Canada. At Master's request, I have been teaching a little Indian girl my way of performing Indian dancing. He felt that the narration combined with the dance made the message understandable for everyone. My schedule is so busy with my own yoga classes, meditation and other spiritual practice, that it was difficult to find a time. Only the hour from 12 to 1—the hottest hour of the day—seemed to be free to teach little Parvati.

Today Master and all the people around him became our audience. "You feel very hot?" he asked. I must have looked like a boiled crab.

"You want rain?"

I laughed, "A little rain to cool off would not be a bad idea."

"Then let us have some rain," he said. "How long will it take to teach her this dance?"

"At least a week," I answered.

"So let's have some rain each day for the next week at this hour."

Ten minutes later a fine rain started. Coincidence? Surely he cannot command the rain!

A new Western visitor arrived. She introduced herself as the wife of the architect, Mr. Stein. Obviously he was well-known in their home town, but here it didn't mean anything to any of us. She behaved very dramatically, she dressed very dramatically and she wore very heavy makeup.

"At Master's request I have been teaching a little Indian girl
my way of performing Indian dancing."

Everybody who met her asked her if she was an actress. She denied this vehemently, saying that she did not think actresses were very moral women. She obviously did not want to be put into that category. In her company was her 10 year-old son, who did not appear to be a child but rather a little man.

Swami Paramananda dodged all her requests to see Gurudev immediately, saying he could not be disturbed but he would make sure she could meet him next morning. Reluctantly she resigned herself to that. To make her feel a bit at home in these surroundings, so very different from what she was obviously used to, I asked her about her travels, what brought her to India, how she met Swami Sivananda. I told her of the custom of meeting the Master every morning in the office and that one could tune into his vibrations and that there was also an opportunity to ask him questions. She corrected me at once and said, "But I have a private interview with him tomorrow morning. Swami Paramananda has already told me so."

The office was pretty packed when Swamiji arrived with Mrs. Stein to introduce her to Gurudev. She was offered the chair right across from his desk, and she realized that this was somewhat an honour, since this was the chair that was reserved for visitors. Swamiji made some polite inquiries about her travel time and asked her if she would like some tea, coffee or milk. She said she would like some coffee. Swamiji, who knows Master's procedures, left immediately and in a short time came back with the coffee and a box of cookies. She said in a dramatic tone, "Oh, no. I will not eat any cookies. I want to be beautiful for you."

The rest of the people in the office did not know if they should laugh or not. Gurudev had no choice but to listen to her long narrative about her various flights and of how everything was just perfect "because I am always in harmony and God provides for me. I am at peace with myself and I have my ego under control and so have good vibrations. Even if we drive our car in town, if I am in the car we always get a parking place. If my husband cannot get any tickets for the opening of the opera, I will get them. There is nothing that I wish for that does not happen sooner or later. I know all the teachings. I know what it is all about. God provides for me."

Gurudev's smile looked rather amused to me. I think he had to make a great effort not to burst into laughter. But then this smile disappeared. He said something in Hindi to Swami Paramananda who informed her that Master had arranged service to her room for hot water for a bath and special food. She turned around, looked at the others who were sitting on the floor and said, "You see, God provides for me. When you are in harmony, everything comes your way. It manifests."

After she had left Gurudev addressed the rest of us, making perfectly clear that it is not necessarily God's grace that provides everything but it is rather a kind of elemental being of a much lower level of consciousness who, once invoked, has to be kept busy and will become demanding. This kind of practice can bring about a lowering of the consciousness to the level of these elementals. It would be a very great mistake indeed were one to use God's power for so much self-gratification and self-glorification. Gurudev looked with great intensity into my eyes. Maybe he wanted to make sure I understood what he was talking about.

Then he had the swami standing next to his desk tell us a story of a king who had been given the power to order those elementals for his service. They produced everything that the king wanted. They were back so fast that he could not quickly enough express another desire. He became aware that the elementals would kill him if he were suddenly to dispose of their services. The king became desperate. He could not think of anything more that he wanted so he pulled out a hair from his long curly locks and gave that to the elemental genie and said, "Straighten this out." It could not be done, so the king now had a chance to take some rest and think how he could escape from this curse.

After the story was finished, Gurudev had something more to say about it, "Yes, God will meet your needs when you put yourself into His service. You don't have to ask. He already knows what you need. He provides the mother with the milk before the baby is born. He does things in His own time and we have to wait. We have the unfinished hospital building right here at the ashram. It would be a mistake for us to direct God's divine energy to finish it, even though it will have a great purpose, taking care of the sick. God cannot be rushed and hurried. Even to have the hospital finished is a personal ambition for which one could employ those lower nature forces, but one must be perfectly clear who is supplying the help. What are these forces? Not all the time when we think our needs are met does the force come from the Most High. The necessity for discrimination is absolutely essential and cannot be stressed enough."

17 *October*

It is a big handicap not to know Hindi or Tamil. I must miss at least 75 percent of what Gurudev says, although I can read much from his face and tone of voice. This morning he and some other swamis seemed to be having some fun. I assumed from their looks and their smiles that the conversation was about me. I was very curious, but could make out nothing. Suddenly Master started singing and looked straight at me, "Oh my Radha, Oh my Radha, darling Radha, honeyqueen." The whole office roared with laughter. It infected me too, although I had no idea what it was all about.

Later Swami Paramananda told me I was to have afternoon tea with Master in his kutir. Gurudev was sitting as usual in his soft chair in which he could rest. Suddenly he asked me what kind of Indian names I like.

"I don't know any," I said.

"You should have an Indian name."

"Why don't you give me one? Any name you give me would be all right."

He said, "Meditate on it."

Something dawned on me and, with all my concentration, I fixed my eyes on him. "Give me back my old name." I seemed to have taken him by surprise.

"Radha," he blurted out.

All the swamis laughed, and I was pleased to think that I had made him say the name.

Later, when the swamis had gone, I asked Gurudev, "What does Radha mean?"

"Radha means cosmic love. Love all who come in contact with you. Be a spiritual mother to all." He closed his eyes. Was he meditating? I did not know. I closed my eyes too. After some time I felt wonderfully light, weightless. That which seemed to be "I" dissolved. From Gurudev came great waves, filling every cell. I seemed to become bigger and bigger, to extend in all directions. Any moment I will fill the whole world, I thought. What will happen? A feeling of uncertainty forced me to open my eyes. Mine met the Master's, which were looking at me with an indescribable expression of love. Now I know what cosmic love is, I thought. Although I had said nothing, he smiled and nodded his head, yes, yes.

When I left his kutir I was walking on clouds. Unable to talk to anyone, I went straight to my kutir. Not long afterwards someone knocked on my door. It was Ayyapan. "Do you want to go for a walk?" I didn't really want to, but perhaps it was best to go with him, before someone else came and made demands.

In the jungle I told Ayyapan, "Master wants me to choose an Indian name. Which one shall I take?"

"You should meditate on it and then take your old name."

"Ayyapan, you are joking."

"Not at all. You adapt yourself with such speed, you move with such certainty I cannot help but think that you were an

Indian in a previous birth. Master said so to me on the very first day you were here, even before you had dressed in a sari."

I said, "But how can I meditate on names when I don't know any? Help me to find one."

Ayyapan was silent, but when at sunset he suggested we go back, he said, unexpectedly, "I can think of no other name for you than Radha."

Before satsang I found Venkatesananda and said to him, "Since Radha seems to have been my name, I would like to know the story behind it." With his sweet smile, he stopped what he was doing and invited me to sit down. Then he began.

"According to tradition, Radha was a mortal, married, with children. She was a worshipper of Lord Krishna, so sincere and explicit in her devotion that she was bound someday to have spiritual experiences with Lord Krishna Himself. The tears of her deep longing and devotion turned the wooden beads of her mala into pearls. One day Lord Krishna sent His messenger to ask her for a pearl from her mala. She did not want to destroy her mala and reduce the beads from the holy number of 108, so she told the messenger she could not do so.

"After some time the messenger returned again with the same request and Radha gave the same answer. This time the messenger added that the Lord wanted the pearl because He wanted to grow a pearl tree. 'Nonsense,' Radha objected, 'no one can grow a pearl tree.' Lord Krishna's messenger looked at her earnestly and said, 'You forget that nothing is impossible for the Lord.' Radha considered this and then in a quick inspiration took her mala from her neck, handed it to the messenger and said, 'Give Him the whole mala.'

"Radha continued her worship of Lord Krishna. Time passed and the messenger came back again. Now he asked her to follow him because Lord Krishna was going to show her the pearl tree. Radha's pride was hurt that she should be thought so stupid as to believe this and she thought that if she went she would be just laughed at and ridiculed for her naivete. But another part of her was also very curious so she followed the messenger.

"When they reached a grove in the forest, Lord Krishna beckoned her to come closer, and the trees bent back to make an opening. There in the center of it was the pearl tree, shimmering and shining. Radha was astounded. She could barely believe what she saw. Then Lord Krishna took one of the pearls from the tree and added it to the 107 of Radha's mala, to once more complete it and, turning to her, he put the mala around her neck.

"It is interesting," Venkatesananda continued, "that the cross that you gave Gurudev has the colors of Radha and Krishna—black onyx with gold edges signifying the anguish and purity of her longing—and the significance of the pearls on it you now know."

18 October

Venkatesanandaji met me

by the Ganges and invited me to come into his kutir. My eyes wandered over his table. There were letters typed by him concluding "Thy own Self." I felt I must get to the root of this. I have heard, "If I have a thorn in my heart I have to take it out." So I asked him, "Swamiji, did you write these letters?"

"Yes, I work for the Master."

At least he did not lie. I continued, "You mean he signs letters he hasn't written? I am very much irritated."

He smiled at me, "No, no, don't be irritated. No reason for that. Let me tell you a little experience. One night I was tired after writing some 30 letters. As there was only one left, I did not want to keep it for the next day. Because I was tired, my thought-stream with the Master had come to an end, but I applied my will power and wrote the last letter. Next day I muddled it up with all the others. Gurudev signed letter after letter until he came to that particular one. Without a glance he gave it back to me. 'Don't write when you are tired,' he said, 'Write a new one.' Now I ask you, how do you explain that?"

I remembered experiences in Canada when I had given answers to people on problems that I was puzzled about myself. Once or twice the answer was even contrary to my own conviction. Swami Venkatesananda's story and my own experience seem to indicate that Gurudev can transmit his thoughts through another person who is open to be a channel. Next opportunity I must ask him about these things.

I remembered something else. I started to ask Swamiji, "Do you recall a German lady who was here at the ashram a few years ago..." but before I could go any further, he said, "You mean Mrs. Wagner. She not only deserted the Master, but she did some terrible things."

I said, "If he is a guru, how can he make such mistakes?"

"Why say it is a mistake? Do you doubt Jesus Christ because he was deserted and betrayed by Judas? These things need to happen—only then can we see the greatness of a master. Of course, if he takes revenge then he is no saint or guru. But if, like Christ, he submits to the will of God completely, accepts everything, even the greatest trials, and still carries out his mission, still sees God in all, then we can know that he is truly a saint. But you should ask him yourself. His answer will be of greater importance to you."

But I was still wondering, what if he is not my guru? Would he answer frankly, "So far only can I help you, I am not your guru"?

After satsang Gurudev was about to disappear into his kutir when he unexpectedly came back and asked me, "Do you want cocoa?" I didn't really want anything, but I hoped this might be my opportunity to clear up this guru question. I followed him into the little room in front of the kitchen. He put a small table between himself and me and told the cook to make the cocoa.

I moved the table. "I don't want anything between you and me, not even this table." Then I went straight to the point. "Tell me truthfully, are you my guru?" I felt excited, keyed up.

The cook came in with some biscuits. Master took one, broke it in two and put half into my mouth. This gesture calmed me, and I continued more quietly, "You told me in a letter that you are my guru. Now that I am here, you don't say a word." Master looked at me with a smile. I did not find it amusing. I was deadly serious. I waited for his answer.

The pause seemed unreasonably long. Then he said, "You are here, so you are my disciple."

Why would he not say plainly, "Yes, I am your guru" or "No, I am not your guru"? I was becoming agitated again. "Many people are here. Does that mean that they are all your disciples? Must the Master always speak in such a mysterious way? Can you not understand that this human ear wants to hear it directly from you?"

Even in my anguish I did not want to appear disrespectful, so I put my palms together in *pranam*. He put his hands over mine and said gently, "Why do you get so excited? Of course I am your guru. How can it be otherwise?" The cook came with the cocoa. "We can put the table back now?" I nodded. "Drink your cocoa," Master said gently. Suddenly I felt very grateful. Life had a purpose, the purpose of God-realization. To build a cathedral of consciousness one needs an experienced architect—Sivananda.

At Gurudev's *suggestion I am taking*
lessons from one of his disciples, Swami Nadabrahmananda,
whom he calls a music guru. I am to go for two or three hours daily
for his instruction in mantra and Indian instruments. Occasionally Swamiji falls asleep. His *gurubhais* (brother disciples)
explained to me that he would sleep only while I was making no
mistakes. As soon as I made a mistake he would be right there.
That proved to be true. However, to my Western mind, to give a
class and fall asleep was not very satisfactory. I was told that Swamiji gets up at 3 o'clock for his *sadhana*. I could see why he would
be tired in the afternoon. He was singing bhajans and playing his
sitar as his spiritual practice. But I had my doubts about the early
hour.

Having become aware that some of the Indians try to impress
Westerners unduly, I was more inclined now to check things out
for myself before I would accept them. I had wondered how people can do with so little sleep and I thought there was something
wrong with me until I found many people take a siesta for a couple
of hours during the day. Master always said that people who sleep
too much cannot achieve anything on the spiritual path. I certainly wanted to advance, so I was curious about how Swami
Nadabrahmananda would do it.

I decided to find out if the swamis were pulling the wool over
my eyes or if he really did get up at 3 o'clock. My classes were in
the afternoon and I had seen him at lunch around 12; he was also
at satsang every night, so maybe he had some secret mantra. This
morning I heard the blind sadhu who always comes to the Ganges
at 3 o'clock. I hurried into my clothes, took a big flashlight, and
made my way up to the Yoga Museum where Swamiji lives. When
I came closer to the building I could hear his voice. Now that I had
reached his door I decided to knock. If he would let me in I would
just sit and listen. He responded quickly to my knock.

Suddenly he grabbed me by my clothes and pulled me into his room. I was very surprised and I saw great anxiety on his face. He slammed the door shut in a hurry behind me, opened the window shutters and, pointing through them, said "Tiger!" Everything happened so fast, I only saw the big animal from the back, loping into the bush.

I sat down to catch my breath and thought about it. I had been almost immediately punished for my curiosity. I really had no right to check on anybody. Swamiji gave me a blanket to sit on and I urged him to carry on his *sadhana*. As he sang the Hari Om prayer, his voice full and deep, I was transported to another state of consciousness.

22 *October*

Until this morning I had no idea what,

if anything, had been done about the material that I had brought as a gift for Sivananda. Gurudev sent a young messenger with a note saying I should come immediately. Two sisters who were teachers in Dehra-Dun, both devoted to Master, had made the cloth into a coat and delivered it this morning. It is well-made and fits him beautifully. He pointed to a note pinned on the front and I came closer to read it. It was a little poem which the sisters had composed.

> *Sivananda, Beloved of Radha*
> *The presentation of her*
> *Tremendous love*
> *In the shape of lovely*
> *Overcoat*
> *Thou hast got to wear*
> *For countless years.*
> *We all greet Thee*

In this new coat
Thou art going to use
Till humanity is merged in Thee.

When I read "Sivananda, Beloved of Radha. . ." I looked up into Gurudev's face and into his eyes, trying to find anything that would convey something of the meaning of this to me. Again there came a very warm light of love into Gurudev's eyes. I was most happy.

* * * * *

"Can you see God in everything?"

"I try, Gurudev!"

"Ah, no more bedbugs for you."

This very pleasant announcement left me puzzled. Bugs are brought from trains and buses, cars and taxis. They live in cracks of wood, in piles of paper. No bedbugs? Impossible! I have tried to keep everything clean, anytime I return to my kutir I check my sari, but I can't seem to avoid them. Yet I am no longer disturbed. The spiritual atmosphere has taken possession of me to such an extent that all my critical thoughts have just disappeared. Now that I come to think of it, I don't even know how this has happened. It is not because of my effort to control my mind, it has just happened that there is no more room for such negative thoughts. They must have been driven out by the divine thoughts inspired by Swami Sivananda. Obviously a guru must have great patience. Many people, when they first come to him, are most enthusiastic. After some time that cools off and they become very critical and some leave on that account. My way is the opposite. I investigate, observe, criticize, sift and sort things out. After a long time understanding will come, and as this grows I put my whole self into it. Once I am in it with head and heart, I will stick to it.

Today I gave the last lesson to little Parvati. It has rained for one hour at noon every day since I started to teach her. This is certainly evidence of his power. Surely this should give me faith.

Just when I begin to feel that I am

on the right track Gurudev shatters my complacency. This morning he started a conversation with, "You can do some work for me in Canada."

I stared at him. "You don't want me here?"

"I want you, but I want you to work for me in America. Over there you can be of greater service to me."

"But I don't understand, Gurudev. What do you want me to do?"

"Start an ashram or school for the divine Teachings of yoga and Vedanta."

I couldn't believe my ears. "I have nothing to give. I don't know Sanskrit. I have read the Gita, but not studied it. I don't know Vedanta. What do I know? It would be the blind leading the blind!"

"Suppose on the hill lies a man nearly dying of thirst. You sit here on the Ganges, with all the water in front of you. Would you deny him a cup of water because you cannot bring him the whole Ganges or explain to him its chemical content?"

"Then go back to Canada and help the people. Gradually your work will spread. Go also to America, travel about. Give classes in hatha yoga, teach pranayama, pray and meditate together, help people to live a divine life, inspire people to sing the Lord's name. Do it with your whole heart and all will benefit. Tomorrow I will give you Mantra Initiation, for yourself and also to give others. There will be a band of fine young men who will help you establish an ashram and you will have to learn to extract work from them."

Immediately my pride reared up and I blurted out, "I don't like to say thank you. I'd rather do things myself."

Gurudev looked amused at the quick response which gave me

The author learning to speak in front of a crowd
to overcome her shyness.

away and then he said, "Would you rather have people paying off their karma through pain? Hard work is the easiest way to pay off karma."

After I had myself under control I said, "Can all karma be paid off by hard work?"

"Not hard work per se, but with the right attitude, with the right thoughts. Reverse your thinking from expecting praise, tangible rewards or gifts. It is like bookkeeping," and he pointed to a swami who was sitting in a corner, "like his bookkeeping. You pay off your debts and you create a balance of good karma."

Then he referred to the saying of Jesus, that those who have their reward on earth have it as name, fame and recognition while those who don't, have something else to look forward to. I was quite excited because I understood what he was saying. "Another degree of samadhi," I interjected. Master nodded his head.

I must have looked as frightened as I felt, for he added, "I will give you a special blessing. Go now and rest."

But what does it mean, Mantra Initiation? Am I ready for it? I don't feel ready. How can he think I could go back to Canada and teach and start an ashram? I have never been able to speak in front of a crowd—six people are a crowd to me.

24 October

I cannot seem to put into words

what I experienced during initiation. It is too personal, too meaningful; words would be too limiting, too ordinary, and yet I must try. Memory cannot be trusted as time goes by.

This morning before office time I was called to Gurudev. He was sitting on a tiger skin near the Ganges and in his hands he held a mala, an Indian rosary, consisting of 108 beads made from seeds of the rudraksha or the tulsi tree. He explained to me that mantra is much more than prayer, it is a power in itself. Like the

Radha receives her Mantra Initiation from Swami Sivananda.
"It joins the Guru and the disciple with bonds of divine relationship
and it accelerates spiritual development."

two Christian prayers, the Lord's Prayer and the Ave Maria, it contains the concentration and faith of the countless devotees who have repeated it through the ages.

The Mantra Initiation joins the guru and the disciple in a divine relationship and it accelerates spiritual development. One collects a treasure of spiritual wealth, whether one wants it or not—even if one breaks away from the guru—because the guru never breaks with the disciple. The disciple may refuse the practice of the mantra, or may break the relationship with the guru. However, the guru, knowing the Divine Law, has a continuing obligation to the disciple. For his own sake, the disciple should never turn away from the guru without permission. At this moment that is unthinkable to me because of the gratitude I feel for the guidance and dedication of my guru.

Several *brahmacharis* were initiated into *sannyas* at the same time, and afterwards fruits and sweets were served in Master's kutir, along with tea, coffee and biscuits. Gurudev blessed everyone in a singing voice.

Suddenly Lila who was sitting next to me, tapped me and said, "Do you hear? He is singing of you!"

I couldn't believe my ears.

"No more birth for Radha! No more birth for Radha!"

I made my way through the crowd to him. "Gurudev," I tried very hard to be heard through all the noise. Once more I said, "Gurudev, you are terrible to make such jokes."

"No joke." Sivananda kept singing his blessings for everyone present. That gave me time to think.

If this is no joke it is an astounding thought. Reincarnation really appeals to me. It gives chances to improve myself and to eradicate whatever sins are there. Life is then like a school—I can graduate from class to class here if I put the effort in, take responsibility for myself, be aware of new desires cropping up. Awareness—*awareness* and *sincerity* seem to be the keys. That is probably what Gurudev meant—it is all up to me. I must not miss the opportunity of this lifetime. What a joyful thought!

Yesterday I received a note from Swami Chidananda that we would visit the leper colony today after lunch. The horrible sight of so many lepers shook my entire being. Parts of their limbs have withered, parts of their faces are gone. For some, where there should be a nose, there is a big hole. Swami Chidananda was talking to them, introducing us as visitors at the ashram. I just sat in a corner and quietly sobbed. I did not know how to handle the situation. I felt a helplessness at this moment such as I have only experienced during the war.

"Radha, why are you crying?" asked Chidanandaji. "Your crying will not help them. Why don't you do something?"

That took me by surprise and helped stem my high-running emotions. "But what can I do?"

"You can chant mantras, do Indian dancing, take their minds off their affliction. They will appreciate your concern." Of course I consented.

Then I began to think about what else I could do and it came to my mind that they were not only sick but poor also. Immediately I began to collect money from the visitors. I collected 127 rupees and handed it to Swami Chidananda. He asked the doctor in charge how many lepers there were. There were 127!

Then Swamiji told them I was going to sing bhajans, chant mantras and do some Indian dancing. There was a moment of silence and then, as if by an invisible command, all the lepers started chanting. Swamiji told me this was their response to my interest in them. I felt very moved, realizing that in spite of their condition they were able to respond so spontaneously and warmly.

On the way back to the ashram this dramatic visit suddenly made it incredibly clear how fortunate I am and I felt a great surge of gratitude. I decided right then and there not to take my "great pains" too seriously.

Saluting the lepers after chanting. "You can chant mantras,
do Indian dancing, take their minds off their affliction.
They will appreciate your concern."

While changing my clothes back in my kutir, I watched an ant trying to make its way up the wall with a big piece of worm several times its size. Time after time it struggled part way up and then fell down again. I began to count the times the ant fell. About the 23rd time it reached its goal. Suddenly it occurred to me that this is what I must do on the spiritual path—try again, no matter how many times I fail. One day I will succeed.

26 October

Many unfinished thoughts

were lingering in my mind. They were coming faster than I could digest them. I have become aware that when there are thoughts lingering in my mind, needing clarification, I find myself by the Ganges, lingering around Venkatesanandaji's kutir. Today his doors were locked. He was out. I had to sort out my thoughts myself. So many lessons to learn—I wonder how many I have missed. It seems all so terribly important—or so I thought.

When Swamiji came into sight with an Indian woman I forgot in an instant what I had come down for. So much for the importance of my problems! Swami Bliss introduced the Indian lady as Tara, telling me she is the housekeeper of Gauri Prasad, Master's legal advisor.

We both seemed to immediately feel a bond. Tara speaks only Hindi so she expressed her acceptance of me through her gestures, her smile, and a shy attempt to caress my arm. On the spur of the moment I decided to run to my kutir to get the small gold cross with the amethysts, the one I had originally bought for Gurudev but that proved to be too small. I handed it to Tara. She was overjoyed. Swami Bliss shared her excitement while Tara talked in cascades of words to him which he had a hard time to translate fast enough. Tara said that she has known me in a past life and her joy is divided between receiving the gift and meeting me again. Swamiji explained the symbology of the cross to her in Hindi and then translated back to me. Tara made her *pranams* searching for a few English words, "Your God is my God."

What great joy and happiness we shared! Unforgettable! In such a spirit I almost got a grasp on Oneness.

When Swamiji saw how well Tara and I got along together, and how much gentleness and affection there was between us, he suggested that as he was planning to take a day off after weeks of intensive work, we would go to a beautiful waterfall near a mountain lake and have a picnic. At this Tara was very happy and took the next boat home to make preparations.

After lunch Swamiji sent word that I should come down quickly to go with him across the Ganges. We had a beautiful walk to the house where Gauri Prasad lived. Tara had prepared the picnic and she insisted on carrying everything herself because Venkatesanandaji is a swami and I am her guest. We were all in good spirits, and went first to the waterfall. What an experience! The water came down some 25 or 30 feet and it had carved a hole into the top of the mountain. One could see the water rush through the hole while seeing the sky at the same time. The sound of the rushing waters was too loud to permit conversation. Nobody felt like talking anyway. The view was too majestic. We settled, all three, for meditation.

Later on we wandered uphill through the forest until we came to what was probably a little crater lake. Swamiji did all sorts of asanas, floating on the water, something that made me very nervous. What if he should sink with his legs all knotted together? However, he had great fun. I had difficulty in relaxing because I cannot really swim. Tara did not go into the water and I was happy that she kept me company. Every now and then we would look at each other and it seemed that we had a kind of silent conversation. Swamiji came out of the water and we had our picnic. He suggested taking some photos, so Tara and I will have some nice memories of each other.

Radha and Tara embracing. "Radha is my sister. She will not be here for long and I will lose her again."

The day with Tara has made me wonder
—what is the mind? Gurudev also remembers a past life with me. How strange! The idea of reincarnation is very appealing to me. It seems to answer many questions—makes pain and hardship more acceptable. I don't know where to begin to sort it out, but that blissful swami, Venkatesananda, is ever ready to lend a listening ear.

This morning when I came down to the Ganges, Tara had just arrived on the boat. Swamiji had sent word to her that the film was developed and prints made. Some of the pictures had come out very well, but Venkatesanandaji and I discovered that in one of them Tara looked very sad, as though she were crying. He asked her about it and she explained that she had been feeling sad because, "She is my sister. She will not be here for long and I will lose her again. I would feel better if I could go with her and look after her. She came into this life with not very good health."

Swamiji translated. I said, "Does she realize that the country I come from is a very different world, far away?" He translated that but all Tara did was caress my hair and pat my hand. Swamiji told her to come as often as her duties would permit, to be with me. Gauri Prasad, her employer, was often away on legal business, so this will not be too great a problem.

Today, since we were going to the temple at Gita Bhavan, she asked if she could cross on the same boat to have a little time with me. This would not cause any difficulty. We all followed Gurudev down to the boat, got in and sat down. There was a lot of chatter as people settled themselves. Swami Chidananda, knowing that Master was not in favor of that, started to sing a kirtan. Everybody stopped talking and joined in. It was very beautiful to cross the river with the voices sounding over the water. The Ganges was flowing smoothly. The boatman is paid by the government, but Western visitors make a habit of giving him a little money which is probably a welcome bonus because of the rather large families that Indians have.

After we arrived at the other side we had a pleasant ten-minute walk to the Gita Bhavan, where there is a temple, beautifully kept gardens and a collection of buildings. The buildings have many small rooms not much bigger than twice the size of a bed, with a window on one side and a door on the other side. They look like American motels, only much more simple, without the luxury. The place seems to be rather clean and well-kept. There are a couple of swamis living there who do the work. At regular times people would appear at the temple to hear various pandits, scholars or swamis expound and explain the Gita.

The Gita Bhavan is open four months a year, but those who look after everything live there year round. In the fore-room of the temple there are pictures of saints of the many religions of India and there are also pictures of Jesus, Saint Francis and other saints of the Christian church. The Jesus picture is obviously Catholic as it shows a red heart exposed in His chest. I could not for a moment imagine the reverse situation, Lord Krishna's image in a Christian church.

Master asked me how I liked the place. I think I showed my enthusiasm a little bit too openly. Swami Chidananda saved the situation by saying, "Yes, here are beautiful gardens, lots of accommodation and conveniences, but there is no Master."

I immediately got the hint and corrected myself to Gurudev by saying I would not want to miss the spiritual gifts I received from him in Sivananda Ashram, and the beauty of the place could not balance that. We all came together onto the steps of a huge gate and the photographer, Swami Saradananda, took a picture. I sat on Gurudev's left side. Then we all moved to the temple where there were several images of gods and goddesses. In the center was Siva, on the left side Radha and Krishna and on the right Ram and Sita. A gardener explained that the clothes of the images were changed at different times of worship and told us that everything was handmade. I had one of my usual hundred questions.

I asked Swami Chidananda, who was closest at the moment, why all these images were dressed like human beings. At first Swamiji showed what appeared to me to be annoyance, but he seemed to remember quickly that I could not possibly know, so very patiently he explained that the feelings and the love and devotion of a devotee found their expression in this way. The decorating of the images symbolizes how beautiful the Lord is, and this beauty finds its expression in the Truth.

This made me wonder if this is the reason some churches in Europe are almost overloaded with decorations. Is this meant to give sort of a taste of heaven? Then the heaven of the Protestants indeed must be a very poor and lonely place.

Somebody told Gurudev what the time was and I realized this meant we would return to the ashram. I was hanging behind, moving on slowly, absorbed in my own thoughts, but I hurried as soon as I saw that almost everybody was in the boat. I didn't want to keep them waiting. Again we had a boat kirtan. While I appreciated being at Sivananda Ashram and learning from Gurudev and the disciples, I also enjoyed Gita Bhavan and its beautiful surroundings.

28 October

When Master came out of his kutir

this afternoon he had with him a couple from Kashmir. When he saw me he said, "Doesn't she look like a Kashmiri?" He turned to the wife. "You should put her into some of your clothes and fix her hair and let me see if she looks like a Kashmiri. Do you have the pictures?"

The husband handed me two pictures, color slides. There in the photograph was the temple that I had been trying to find for so long, a temple I had first seen years ago in a dream and later it had come to me in meditation. Now I understood the joke that Master had made which I had thought was silly, "Meet my friend from Kashmir." So Gurudev had known all along of the experience I had had — obviously a past life experience that had taken place in Kashmir — and he had asked this couple to bring a photo of the temple so that I would know it was real.

The Kashmiri couple were of course eager to hear the story. "Several times I had an experience where there was a beautiful temple exactly like the one here in the pictures. I wore clothes that were not saris, but skirts, something like yours. In the experience I came down these steps here and I wanted to leave and go to the other shore. But somebody called me back, somebody in authority, saying that the job was not done and I could not leave. Otherwise, he said, I would be like a person who goes to sit down at a table loaded with food, knowing that I had left behind people who were much in need of such food. I was sad that I had to stay."

Gurudev inserted a remark here that one can never leave if the job is not finished. I looked at him with a question mark on my face but I knew he would not say more and I would have to figure this out for myself. We all went to the office.

While I was eating supper later on, one word was repeating itself over and over in my mind. Reincarnation. It is obviously a fact. What other explanation could there be for this and for my feelings about Tara? Glimpses like these from previous lives — could it be that one dips for a moment into the sea of time?

As I was walking home from the market at Lakshmanjula I saw an old man lying on the road exposed to the fierce sun. Was he dying? No one seemed to be helping him and when I showed concern, everyone looked at me with blank faces saying, "Karma" or "His time is up." I hurried back to the ashram for help but all I could get was a container from a swami which I filled with water. Then I went back the three miles to the old man. I tried to open his mouth and pour the water in. People were gathering around, talking and gesticulating, probably partly because the old man's loin cloth had come apart and he was entirely uncovered, but I did not care. It was more important to me to give him help. Finally a couple of Indians came and carried him away.

On the way back to the ashram I pondered about death. No birth without death. Is death the beginning or the end? Is it the indication of a new birth? What happens between death and rebirth?

29 *October*

After breakfast I could see from my window that a group of people had gathered in front of the office, so I went down to find what it was all about. A swami had a message for us from Gurudev. We were all to stay within the compound of the ashram and not to go beyond for any reason because there was a rabid dog in the vicinity who had bitten a number of people. Swamiji made it very clear that we must obey these instructions and not even go for meditation to our favorite places if they were not on ashram ground. He specified exactly the area where we were safe.

"Does this mean we are now protected by Master?" a visitor asked. Swamiji confirmed this, impressing on us that we should make very sure that everybody understood Master's orders. I considered that this must be the radius of Gurudev's aura.

Swamiji then went around to make sure everyone stayed in their place. Later in the afternoon he was still looking for a *gurubhai* who kept his meditation place secret so he would not be disturbed.

30 *October*

This morning the ashram was in a great commotion. The missing swami had indeed not got the message and after his meditation, while walking back to the ashram area, a dog came towards him wagging its tail, seeking affection. He patted it in response. Suddenly the dog sunk its teeth into his forearm and he had to wrestle with it to shake it off. Immediately he made his way to the ashram doctor and, for the first time, heard about the rabid dog. Dr. Roy informed Gurudev who alerted the doctors of the hill station, Roorkie, to locate serum. When that was done Dr. Roy rushed the swami there in a taxi.

Dr. Roy has now been away almost

a week. He has left phone messages for Gurudev almost daily at the post office, the only place with a telephone. We were all relieved when Dr. Roy finally announced Swamiji's improved health and today a telegram arrived saying they were on their way back to the ashram by taxi.

To celebrate the good news, Gurudev ordered special food and special *prasad* to be prepared for satsang as a thanksgiving from all of us. Two hours later Dr. Roy phoned again to say that when, after loading the car, he went to get the swami, he found him sitting cross-legged on his bed as in meditation. He spoke to him and touched him on the shoulder but got no reply. Then the doctor checked his breath, his heart and pulse and discovered that the swami had left his earthly body. They put him into the taxi and brought him back to the ashram.

Why didn't Gurudev know he was going to die? Why didn't the swami know of Gurudev's order to stay within the confines of the ashram?

I don't like to think about death. So many people die because of physical violence. History is full of wars and killing, of disease and disasters when many innocents are the victims of the fanaticism of others. Mankind with all its intelligence, education, knowledge and science does not seem to have found reasonable ways of settling disagreements.

This swami had given Gurudev many years of selfless service. He was gentle and understanding. There are plenty of parasites misusing and abusing Gurudev's generosity. Why wasn't one of them bitten by the dog? Animals are supposed to have such good instincts. What happens to the instincts when a dog gets sick? Is it not attracted by the kindness of one who would help? My mind can produce more questions than it can answer.

There are special meditations on death where disciples are asked to spend a night in a cemetery, sitting on a corpse. I haven't been asked to do that. I don't know if Gurudev has ever ordered anyone to do so. But I certainly have been stimulated to think about death. I knew this swami, even though I never could recall his unpronounceable name. I wish I could know the time of my death.

6 *November*

In great sadness the ashram made

the preparations for the funeral. To my surprise I found Gurudev in his office working as usual. I had to ask him, "Gurudev, this swami has given you 18 years of service and you don't even go to his funeral? I don't understand."

He looked at me seriously and said, "The priest will take care of the body. I take care of the soul." I understood this immediately.

Then Master said, "You go and see your funeral."

I looked at him and asked, "Am I soon going to die?" He did not answer, just went back to his work. I walked down to the Ganges. They had wrapped the body first in the white cloth the swami had received at initiation into *brahmacharya*, then in other cloths with certain spiritual insignia, and finally in a rough cloth with a lot of stones to weigh it down. It was put into a boat, taken to the middle of the river and lowered into the Ganges. Prayers and sutras were recited. Chanting was going on the whole time.

My mind was pondering the mystery of life and death. How long will I live? Will there be enough time left to do the job of development that will open the door of realization? Always more questions. One answered, ten others appear. I have moments when I think I have begun to understand something, but obviously death can come fast anywhere at any time.

Before satsang Dr. Roy related all that had happened, including the difficulties of bringing the body back to the ashram. The taxi driver did not want to drive a corpse and it took a large number of rupees to convince him. Other swamis spoke of their *gurubhai*. Then Gurudev said a few words about what a wonderful swami he had been, reliable, hard-working, what wonderful service he had given. He finished by saying, "I am very sad in my heart. We have lost a valuable member of the ashram and a worker who will not be easily replaced."

Gurudev accompanied by Swami Satchitananda. Radha calls
Satchitananda "Christmas Tree" because he carries around things
that Master might need, including sweets for the children.

The mad dog is shot! A farmer who has a permit for a gun to defend his cattle against wild beasts was able to track down the dog and shoot him. The man arrived at the ashram with the dead dog just as Master was about to close his office. Master praised him and ordered Swami Satchitananda (I call him Christmas Tree because he carries around bags of things Master might need) to give the farmer some money as a reward. But no, this was not what he wanted. Finally he said, twisting his Ghandi cap in embarrassment, "I want a picture with you and the dog." Master immediately obliged and the man went off happy.

* * * * *

This afternoon Gurudev sent for me. He was sitting on one of the low stone walls. I walked over, gave him my *pranam,* and he showed me a very big enlargement of a picture where he and I are sitting in a car. I am wearing my white silken sari, his gift to me, with the pallu over my head according to Indian tradition. The door of the car is wide open, so we can both be well seen sitting in the back.

"Oh, my God," I said, "Don't hold it up so high! All the people behind can see. Don't you know there is already a great deal of gossip calling you the Maharaja and me the Maharani? I think the boys who work in the dark room must have helped to spread this talk."

Master waved this aside. He couldn't care less, but he obliged by lowering the picture. Then he looked at me. I had a sense of expectation. What was he going to say?

"How does the picture look to you?" he asked.

I said, "Well, I can see why they call us the Maharaja and the Maharani, but everybody knows you are my guru and I am your disciple."

Master took my hand and started walking. He looked at me and said, "Now, Radha, what kind of a walk is this?" I had no idea. "This," Gurudev helped me out, "is a spiritual marriage—you and I walking together."

I wasn't quite sure if he said walking or working and I did not dare to ask. I saw the disappointment in his face that I did not understand. Was it ignorance, stupidity or lack of sensitivity? I did not know. I felt just as sad as the expression on his face. I looked at Gurudev because he had stopped walking and I said, "You must be very lonely. Even I, who am tuned in to you, let you down again and again. I can't grasp things, I can't understand." We walked back the short distance. Master did not say another word, which increased my discomfort.

Many people began to gather around but I did not feel like being part of the group. There was something more important to do, to think, to let my intuition emerge. Anything that he has said up until now is burned into my mind because every time he speaks I take great pains to understand what he truly means. It becomes more and more obvious to me that those who do listen and try to carry out what they hear have his greatest attention and guidance.

9 *November*

This afternoon *a group of teachers* arrived with their students and wanted to do a spiritual play as a gift to the Master and entertainment for the ashram members. There was a half hour delay so Swami Chidananda took matters into his own hands and told in English, to the three or four

Swami Sivananda looking at photograph. "I can see why they call us the Maharaja and the Maharani, but everybody knows you are my Guru and I am your disciple."

hundred people who had gathered, the story we were going to see.

Suddenly across the place there rolled a powerful *Om*. Everybody was silent. There was no doubt that *Om* came from Gurudev. He scolded Swamiji in front of everybody. "What is this nonsense? You have no humility. Who gave you the order?"

I was shattered. This was just more than I could take. I felt very deeply for Swamiji. I walked over to Gurudev, shook my head and said, "Gurudev, I don't understand."

In a low voice he said, "He is a strong soul. He is a diamond already. What I do is a little polishing because I care."

Then I realized that by long ingrained habit I identified with Swami Chidananda rather than my Higher Self, and what I identified with was this personality aspect within me that likes to be so agreeable and often indulges in self-pity. Chidanandaji took things in his stride, bowed to Master and kept silence.

I gave Master my *pranam,* and removed myself from the collected audience to reflect on my thoughts and feelings.

10 November

Gurudev sent a young boy to take me

to a place where pieces of material and carpets were spread on the ground near one of the big trees. Master was not in his usual clothes. As soon as I arrived he proceeded to demonstrate asanas to me because he had been telling me that I must go to the hatha yoga classes. I had objected that, as a performing artist, I had moved my body sufficiently and even added, in the heat of the moment, "You are too fat. I don't believe you can do any of them yourself." He probably thought that he could convince me only by accepting the challenge.

Fortunately I had my camera with me and after I had taken

some shots I said, "Well, I have to change the film. I would like to have a picture of you in the lotus posture." I was convinced that he could not sit in the lotus posture. The changing of the film took my attention away from him and when I aimed the camera at him again there to my surprise Gurudev, with a very mischievous smile on his face, was sitting in the lotus posture, curious as to how I would react. I was happy that he had taken it in good humor. We both laughed.

After this morning's performance, he talked to me about the importance of the practice of hatha yoga in order to penetrate the deeper levels. I started thinking and said, "Gurudev, can you give me one asana as an explanation? I don't know where to search, where to begin. I am totally unaware of what you are talking about."

He selected the headstand. "When you stand on your head, you have already learned of the physical benefits, but now imagine again that you are standing on your head. What else can you observe?"

I tried in my imagination to put myself in that position and I said, "Well, everything is upside down."

"Very good, very good." Master said. "And what is upside down? Tell me all about it."

"Well, my immediate surroundings, everything that is within the vision of my eye, and that is as far as I can observe."

Master said, "How does that apply in life?"

I didn't know what he was talking about so again he had to help me out by saying, "People have opposed you, haven't they?"

"Oh, yes, plenty."

"They believe the opposite to what you believe. Well, the headstand can help you by making you your own opponent."

"How is that done?"

"You take your cherished beliefs, go right in the opposite direction just as you would oppose another person. If you can do this, the result will be a greater accuracy of what you believe to be true, a better balance. You will not be flustered, you will not be angered if anybody opposes you."

I could see that, too.

"You will have a much better centered position. You will also not be so foolish as to say that you have all the answers." Then Master said, "You have seen the Yoga Museum. You know where the chakras are located, from the pictures there?"

"Roughly. I have had no classes or instructions yet."

So Master said, "From the top of the head comes down the nectar and the ambrosia."

I focused my attention on his face with great intensity. He said, "The first chakra, the Muladhara, is the seat of passion and is like a big fire. All the divine insights, the nectar and ambrosia, are lost in the fire of passion, just as when water is poured on fire, it steams off."

He continued, "So if your head is in the clouds, that is not very helpful. If your feet are on the ground, they are glued to the earth and you are trapped in the power of the earth, but if you turn yourself upside down, your feet are rooted above in heaven and the mind becomes stable. Now the fire has no chance to burn the nectar and ambrosia because the Muladhara is above the Sahasrara, or seventh chakra."

Then there was a long pause. Master indicated that he wanted to go for a walk and I could go along. I would rather run to my room, get out my diary and write everything down, but I decided that I had better stay with him. We walked along the Ganges, this time not in the direction of Rishikesh, but rather in the opposite direction, which meant that the Ganges now flowed towards us. We came upon a little clearing and Gurudev pointed to a building of which we could only see the roof. Around the building there was a stone wall. Master proceeded down a footpath to this building and he pointed to a door on which was written in English in big letters, "I have not looked into a woman's face for 30 years. I give no dharshan. Leave me alone."

Gurudev looked at me quizzically and said, "Are you impressed?"

"No, not at all. Poor man, how fearful, how afraid he must be if the very sight of a woman could disturb his peace and create this fire of passion that you just talked about in the first chakra."

Gurudev's face was very happy. He looked like a hen with a little chick, very proud that it has learned a lesson.

We walked back to the ashram on the other side of the road where the mountains sloped. There was a small gorge with water coming down. In the past there was probably a great mass of water but now there was an open space in which people had built a small square water tank, not more than 4 feet across and between 3 and 4 feet high. We held our hands under the water that was gushing into this tank and drank from them. The rim of the tank had an opening lip formed by small stones which allowed the water to run out in many directions, so the area around the tank was very lush and green from this simple irrigation system. There were a number of plants and flowers here that I had not seen before. Six or eight people had come along and joined us. After Gurudev, we all refreshed ourselves by dipping our hands into the water to cool off our wrists.

Master said, "You see, if this tank were not collecting the water and then directing it, what you admire here would not exist. The water would just run off, probably even damage the road, taking everything towards the Ganges."

He looked at me very intently. I knew that he wanted to know if I understood. I had the habit of mentally repeating his words so that I could focus on them to discover the deeper meaning. I was still wrapped up in my thoughts of what he had just said when he turned and started to move towards the ashram. Obviously I was not yet in the habit of seeing the symbolic meaning, or rather the meaning in each symbol, that gave the clue to the message, because almost immediately he stopped, faced me again and said, "What is a different kind of energy? Energy is neutral. Energy directed is a blessing, undirected. . ." He looked at me without finishing his sentence and, of course, I had by now got it.

I asked him if I could do the asanas in my room without going to the class since in order to understand its symbolic meaning, it would be necessary to hold a position over a long time. In the hatha yoga class I would have to follow the instructor. Gurudev seemed to sense that I had other reasons and point-blank he asked me, "Why do you not want to go to hatha yoga in the morning?"

I told him that the room was so full of people and everybody collected around me, sometimes asking who could be on the right and left of me. Swami Vishnudevananda is an excellent teacher, but people don't come to learn from him, rather to see us Western women. Vishnudevananda, who has offered to pose for some pictures that the photographer swami (Saradananda) is going to make for me to take along when I return to North America, knows my true reasons. I said, "In the West we are more used to seeing a body exposed and pay no attention to it, but here it seems to be different."

Master understood and said that I could practice in my room and let him know when I thought I had found the deeper aspects of different asanas. He said, "You must discover these in at least six asanas. They can be your own choice."

11 November

"In half an hour a function

is going on in my kutir. You too can come," Sivananda told me as he left his office yesterday.

I went to my kutir to refresh myself with some cold water and change my sari. As I was coming back I met Swami Chidananda, who told me that some devotees wanted to celebrate Pada Puja before their departure.

I decided to stay close to Swamiji in the hope of gathering

from him some details of the meaning of this celebration. He guessed my thoughts and while preparation was going on, explained all about the ceremony in a low voice. "Pada means feet. Puja means prayer. Prayer at the Master's feet is a symbolic way for the devotee to express love, gratitude and devotion to the Master. The feet washing as an Eastern custom is known to you from the Bible. It is still done in India.

"But, Swamiji, why does he look so bored? That is not very respectful to the people who honor him that way."

Chidanandaji smiled. "That is the way it looks to you, Mataji. But we would lose faith in the guru if he were impressed with the worship. A normal person would be conceited about it, because he would take it all personally, while the true meaning is that the guru serves only as a visible picture for the invisible. Concentration on the Highest is easier when we fix our minds on something we can grasp, like the living form of the guru."

"But can devotion and respect not be expressed differently?"

"Of course, but what you witness here comes from the old traditions of this country. Respect for elders is still expressed in this way in some families, and so the man of today can, in addition to devotion and respect, check his *ego*. Not all of our own people will perform this Puja; some feel they are too modern. That is what they think, while the real reason is that their ego prevents them from doing so."

Unknowingly (or was it knowingly?) Swamiji had touched a sore spot in me. I know I would never be able to do such Puja. My pride would not permit me to bow down to any living person's feet.

When flowers were placed on Master's feet by the couple who performed the Puja, Swamiji whispered, "Flowers are used as symbols of devotion." When milk was poured over Gurudev's feet, he again whispered, "Milk is a symbol for wisdom. All who gather around a Master receive his wisdom. Nothing is meant for the human body." So many new things, so many strange things— very bewildering.

After Puja, Master gave a manuscript to me written in German with the request to translate it for him as fast as possible — a difficult job for one who is not at home in the English language. I worked on it till nearly 2 a.m. Naturally I slept late in the morning. But the manuscript was not the only cause for that.

About an hour after I went to sleep something woke me up. Something moved over my head like a caress. I guessed that it was another Western lady who usually comes to my room to pick me up. When I called her name, there was no answer. Drowsily I said, "The temple bells have not rung yet. You've come early. I went to bed late, let me rest a little longer." Still no reply.

Suddenly I felt clearly that the something moving over my hair was not a human hand. I opened my eyes. Right down my forehead hung the long tail of a big rat! At first I was horrified. I brushed it off. It ran down my blanket. Suddenly it turned, as though it wanted to have a good look at me. We fixed our eyes on each other. I realized that, after all, a rat is not such a terrible thing. This one had nice shiny little eyes. But I was tired, too tired for rats, so I pushed it off the bed and went back to sleep.

At 7:00 I got up and retyped my translation and had just finished when I saw Gurudev with a small group of people proceeding to his office. I rushed into my sari and went down.

Master offered me the visitor's chair. Surprised I asked, "Am I still a visitor? I thought I was now one of the ashram family!" Master did not take any notice of my protest. "Take this seat." I did. Long silence while he took up some work.

Suddenly he looked at me, "Can you see God in everything?" I was perplexed. Did he know of my experience with the rat, or was this a coincidence?

"At least," I said, "I try, as long as you don't come with anything bigger than rats." All those present in the office laughed and I told of my night's experience. Then I began to wonder, how much do gurus know? How much direct influence do they have?

I can see in my guru a great saint, a channel of great Divine powers. God and Guru are one, say India's teachings. This oneness exists with all, but the difference lies in the fact that the guru knows it, has realized it, while it remains for all others only theory. Whatever the man Sivananda is, however great a puzzle he often appears to be, I can see in his face every now and then a painful expression when I do not understand.

12 November

A little boy brought a note from

Chidanandaji saying that I should come to his kutir at once to clear up something of great importance. I was curious what this could be. It was indeed a matter of great importance. The police have come to inform me that my visa has expired and that I have to leave the country within a week. This is a terrible blow. I had asked for a visa for six months to have sufficient time to study. I was given three with the assurance that prolongation was just a formality. The officer himself was not only polite but also felt very sympathetic.

Chidanandaji comforted me by his promise to try everything possible. "The Master has some good friends in the government. We will see, don't lose hope."

But I know the Master does not like to take advantage of his influential devotees, something I have always admired in his character.

Finally the officer had an idea. "You apply again. Keep a copy, so you have proof. Then wait. It will take some time before you get an answer and this way, time extends itself."

I was hopeful again. Surely time will be on my side. In India it takes a quarter of an hour to mail a letter, one to four hours to mail a parcel, one hour to cash a traveller's check, ten hours for a 16 mile train ride. And if this goes all down the line in the government, I will have to wait more than three months for an answer!

Radha making a *pranam* to Gurudev. "The most precious things one must keep in one's heart."

If! If not, then my stay has come to an end. Unimaginable! It just cannot be!

Suddenly I was overpowered by the thought that I will have to go, thrown out of this paradise by some regulations of the country. My voice left me, I could not say a thing. I ran down to Swami Venkatesananda's kutir. "I can't get an extension," I sobbed. "It's all finished!" I could not stop my tears.

"Mataji, if you cry, I also must cry. I cannot see tears. Please take this milk, sit down and let us see what can be done." Swamiji was like a sweet son comforting his distressed mother. It was the first time in my life that I actually burst so suddenly and with such vehemence into tears. Pride has always prevented me from letting anybody become aware of my feelings.

When Venkatesanandaji saw that there was not much he could do, that I just needed time to recover from the shock, he took his veena and played.

Not long ago I was tearing this place to pieces with all my complaints and criticism, now I cannot bear to think that my time is over. I have become absorbed so much in its holy atmosphere and the holy love of Gurudev that now I do not want to go. Everyone has become my brother and sister. I have changed so much. Now I feel sorry for someone who loses his temper with me and I feel like begging him not to injure himself because I realize how much this swami will have to go through in spite of mantra singing and reciting scriptures. Is this really I? Who is this new I? Not the Sylvia I have known for forty-four years. I have been given so much! I have experienced so much! My diary does not tell even a shadow of it.

The past years of my life are just a dream from which I have now wakened. The whole thing is so fantastic, like a fairy story, one dare not tell about it. The most precious things one must keep in one's own heart. Here in this holy atmosphere one cannot help but remember, in one way or other, one's real divine nature. This love I feel now is the reflection of all those who have spent their time with me, helping me. I have found myself a member of a holy family. Holy and happy. Yet they are men like any other. But what awakens this love is their own love for God, to be one with Him. What makes them all so lovable is their sincere struggle, their longing for the Divine, visibly expressed in the love and devotion to the guru. Where is now the jealousy and greediness that had appeared to me at first? Have I put on rose-colored glasses? No, indeed. But I have learned to see the other side of the coin. My attention is now concentrated on the good, the Divine in everyone.

13 November

I have done everything I can.

I have even persuaded Swami Chidananda to write for help to Mrs. Velodi and have enclosed a note myself. Her husband is a high government official so Chidanandaji was really acting against Gurudev's wishes. But I was close to tears when I asked him and so grateful when he agreed.

Afterwards I walked to the police station, which was just a few hundred yards from the ashram, to talk to the officer again. I told him about my worry of getting involved with the law in a foreign country. He was a nice man, waved all this aside and said, "Put your trust in the guru." He gave me a chair, made me a cup of coffee and told me an incredible story about Gurudev.

"It was almost like Gandhi," he began, "you know Gandhi was shot by a man who was convinced that he was doing the right thing to kill him. Well, a fellow came here one day and in the folds of his robes he carried a hammer, big, heavy, such as is used in construction. He had in mind to find an opportunity to bash Gurudev's head in and kill him."

"But why would anybody want to do this?"

"Well," the police officer said, "you know how people are. It is all jealousy. As you well know, Gurudev is never entirely alone. There are always a lot of people around, but when there were only a few this man seized his opportunity. Some of the swamis with Gurudev had to wrestle with the man and get the hammer out of his hand. Somebody came running here to the police station. We handcuffed him. Over there," he pointed to the door, "he was locked up for the night.

"Swami Sivananda came the next morning very early and wanted to see the man. My colleagues and I objected because we were afraid that the man would try to harm the Master, but finally we gave in to his desire and let him into the cell. We carefully left the door open so we could keep an eye on the situation. Swamiji handed the hammer back to the man and said, 'Do what you were going to do yesterday.' The man was so startled and we were ready to jump, but he fell at Gurudev's feet, asked for forgiveness and asked to become his follower. One of the devotees at the ashram told me that he had been a really bad character and all he is today he owes to Gurudev." I was amazed when I realized which swami this is.

I thanked the police officer for his kindness and his concern and he assured me once again that everything will be all right, Gurudev will take care of it. But what is one to do when one can muster faith at one time and then at another it is all gone as if it had never existed? How does one maintain faith? Still so many unanswered questions.

I went down to the water to find Swami Venkatesananda. The story of the policeman had filled me with excitement and I needed to talk to somebody about it. Swamiji added some more details, then remarked, "You see, it takes time to understand Gurudev. He is not easy to understand. I have been here for many years now and I still have to think, to ponder, what it is he means. By the way, you remember Master getting sick for three days? Well, yesterday a telegram came from a man saying that he thanks the Master for all he did for him. His wife is now well and healthy."

"But why," I asked, "did Master have to get sick? I have never heard of Jesus getting sick when he healed people. I still don't understand."

"Well, Gurudev found no other solution to help the man, to save the life of the mother of four children. It's like this," he said to me. "Let's assume you owe somebody a great amount of money and you can't pay and you are threatened with prison. Then I come along and offer to take over all your debts. I have to use my own money for this."

I pondered this. It was something to hang onto for a while till I could grow more in understanding. Then he took the veena and played very softly. I don't know if it was the melody, but somehow it spoke to my heart and it seemed to be Swamiji's way of communicating without words. After a few minutes I left because I knew he was very busy.

17 November

It was decided that I should go to New Delhi to stay with the Velodis while I awaited the decision on my visa. At the first meal in their home we all sat in chairs around a huge table that could have been anywhere in Europe. There were two spoons set at my place, which was between Mr. and Mrs. Velodi. The servant carried the dishes around, each individual helping himself to some food or passing it by. When everyone had food on their plates, the master of the house took the first handful.

Already familiar with Indian customs, I ignored the two spoons and did the same. Everybody looked at me. Mr. Velodi asked me who taught me this perfect Indian conduct. I said I was not taught by anybody. He said, "You put your left elbow on the table, you let your hand hang down and you eat with your right hand. This is perfect etiquette."

Swami Venkatesananda playing the veena for his guru. "Then he took the veena and played very softly . . .it seemed to be Swamiji's way of communicating without words."

"I remember my mother having often asked me to write on a piece of paper 25 times, 'I shall not put my left elbow on the table.' "

Everybody laughed and said, "Did you stop doing it?"

"Apparently not," I said, "it was a bone of contention in the family for years."

Mr. Velodi said, "Carry-over from a past life. You must have been an Indian."

Then Mrs. Velodi told the story of my buying the sari in New Delhi, wearing it properly and feeling so much at ease. She said I moved so gracefully in a sari — as if I had never worn anything else.

It has been interesting for me to stay in the house of well-to-do Indians. It is very European in appearance — carpets, furniture, the rooms, except that the ceilings are higher and there is a row of windows at the top through which the heat can escape. The rooms are all quite comfortable. She showed me a room in which her women servants and another in which her men servants live. They each have a locker with a key in which they can keep personal belongings, money and other valuables. It is the best I have seen so far in regard to servants' quarters. In the three days I have been here, Mrs. Velodi and I have got to know each other much better. She is really a very fine woman, good and kind.

This afternoon Mr. Velodi said that I could be sure of receiving the visa from the home office and I could return any time I wanted to the ashram. The visa would be mailed to Swami Chidananda, being the Secretary General of the ashram. I thanked him profusely. I am extremely relieved. And now I find I will have the good fortune of travelling by car with Mrs. Velodi, since she has decided to spend a week at the ashram.

The celebration of the worship

of Divine Mother takes place a few weeks before Christmas. All the little girls in and around the ashram have been gathered together and they are sitting under a big tree. They are worshipped as Divine Mother incarnate. So all the swamis, even those closest to Gurudev, prostrate themselves full length before each little girl. They go from child to child repeating the prostration before each one. Every little girl represents an aspect of Divine Mother Sakti. Somebody reads from the scriptures about the glory of the Divine Mother while this is going on, incense is burned and prasad is distributed. Gurudev is for this day also Divine Mother manifest. To all disciples and devotees he is the spiritual mother who has helped to give birth to the life of the aspirant. After the ceremony the children are taken to Gurudev's kutir where they get cocoa and sweets, things that most of the parents are too poor to buy for the children, so it is a great day for them.

Sri Ramakrishna was a great worshipper of Divine Mother and Gurudev often tells the men, particularly the Western ones who have had plenty of opportunity to be unfaithful in their marriages, to treat every woman as if she were Divine Mother herself. "Every woman that you have coaxed into your bed, even with her consent, in some future life you will have to be her lawful husband and you will meet again and again until the relationship is dissolved in peace and harmony. Reincarnation," Master would clarify, "is very precise and nothing escapes." When the Western man looks at him with a doubting expression on his face, he reminds him that Jesus said you have to account for every jot and tittle. Jesus too knew the Law and suddenly I understand why the disciples would say, "He speaks a hard language. Who can listen to Him?"

I have heard that just before

Christmas there will be four people initiated into sannyas. December and March are the usual times for initiation. The names of three of them are known, but not the other, and people are speculating that I might be the fourth. Perhaps I should feel greatly honored, but this is not my reaction. I feel I am not ready for *sannyas*, the path of renunciation, at all. I stormed in to Swami Bliss' kutir and told him of the rumor. As usual he had a laugh and said, "But why do you worry, and by what means do you know if you are ready? Why don't you leave that to the Master? If he initiates you or plans to initiate you, it is his responsibility. You are making your life more difficult."

While I have to agree in one way, I can't in every way, because I cannot change my nature so fast. I feel that I should be given an opportunity to discuss this, voice my opinion and at least be told what it means to become a swami. When I saw that Swamiji was very busy I decided to leave and think about it. If the Master thinks I am ready — but how could he know for sure? I have only been here for such a short time and I am still far from being a living god on earth, although, apart from some like Swami Chidananda and Swami Venkatesananda, I am by no means convinced yet that I could call most of the swamis living gods on earth.

Later I asked Gurudev about this. He said, "How many people live in the world?"

I said, "I don't know, but I would guess hundreds of millions."

"Well," he said, "more than several hundred million. And how many people out of this many come here? By the very fact that you are seeking God and you put all this effort in, have made all these sacrifices, doesn't this somehow single you out? Aren't you somehow different from people who are only interested in eating, drinking, sleeping, business?"

"Yes, it is true I'm not interested in those things."

"Well, all those who are here I call living gods on earth. Even if somebody can only be a *sannyasi* for a year or for a month, at one moment he had the courage to put his foot on the path. According to the Gita that will provide him with a favorable birth at some other time."

Then Master pulled out of his pocket and handed me a small book, *Necessity for Sannyas.* He must have seen the worried look on my face because he said, "No, you are not the fourth person."

I let out a sigh of relief.

I thought of something else, "Gurudev, the names of Siva and Krishna do not mean anything to me. I think about it and I meditate about it, but I don't get any response despite all efforts. What should I do?" Gurudev kept silent. I did not get an answer.

22 November

I have just read the book

Necessity for Sannyas. It talks about the tremendous power of the mantra. It says here in the book that nobody who is not a *sannyasi* may be present when someone is initiated into *sannyas.* They have their heads shaven. I wonder how I would feel if I were going to be number four and had to have my hair all cut off. I am very sensitive on the head. Some swamis put all those shawls and scarves around their heads, probably to protect themselves from the heat or the cold. Many let their hair grow again afterwards, which I think is much more practical instead of wearing a turban. The necessity for fasting, I have observed, does not seem to be taken too seriously. They just cut down on the general intake of food. I thought fasting was eating nothing, not even fruit juice, just water.

Later on at the office the usual procedure was suddenly interrupted by a middle-aged man who threw his orange robe on the floor in front of Gurudev and shouted at him at the top of his voice. He was terribly angry and he tossed his mala on the desk. This was in front of 50 or 60 people, more than half of them visitors. We all looked at each other, shocked.

Master's face remained stony, unmoved. I ran after the ex-swami because I thought he might be still caught up in a lot of preconceived ideas as I was, and maybe in talking to him I could help him. But he was in no mood and he kept gesticulating and shouting probably in Hindi, and ran off towards the road.

I returned to the office. Master proceeded as if nothing had happened. I could see no expression on his face. I was sitting on pins and needles, eagerly waiting for a moment when I could ask him what was to me a very important question.

"Gurudev," I said with great excitement and very likely my voice sounded accusing, "You are the Master, you are the great yogi, you have the awareness, and if yogis can even disclose past lives to the disciples as I have read in the books, why don't you help him to clear his doubts and make him see?"

Gurudev looked at me for awhile quietly. He did not seem angry at me for asking these questions in front of the visitors. The silence was a little disconcerting for me, and I tried to bridge this by making myself the speaker for all the Western visitors. "Everything is so difficult to understand, particularly the daily experiences which often seem to be in contrast to what we read in the books. They teach complete obedience to a guru; that *sannyasins* are gods on earth; of the guru's great powers; that all the things that happen, happen by the grace of the guru. Yet *sannyasins*, who are given all that worship and reverence and respect, are still very human. And look at what happened here right now."

I turned around to the other visitors and I knew that they felt a relief that I had the courage to voice what was often brought up in conversations. He explained a few things, "The impact of *sannyasa* is not destroyed by his present ignorance. It takes many lifetimes before purity is achieved."

"You mean before selfishness is overcome?" I interrupted.

He nodded his head. "When we are young, we are very foolish. When we get older, we get more insight. He has still many years in this life, and the ideals of *sannyas* will never leave him entirely, regardless of his mistakes. There is always something underground in the mind that remains. Memory can be a curse and a blessing."

I *pranamed* to the Master. I apologized for my behavior and words and I assured him again that I have no intention of being disrespectful to him, even if it might appear so, because of the way my Western temperament expresses itself. Then Master moved his head from side to side, "Adja, adja." I still felt somewhat tense and kept my eyes fixed on Master's face, waiting for a confirming glance that everything was all right and he did understand me.

When lunchtime came and we all got up, Master gave me a few parcels to carry for him, which loving devotees had sent to him, saying, "You can carry this for me," and looking at me very kindly. I was most happy to do that little service. I followed Gurudev to the door of his kutir. Satchitananda opened it from the inside and I handed the parcels to him. Before Master entered, he paused again and looked at me. "The great stories that you read about the illustrious yogis of the past are true. They had worthy disciples. Today we still have great yogis, but there are no capable disciples." With that Master disappeared into his kutir.

After lunch I met Swami Ramananda and we had a little chat. Swamiji wore a mala of very big beads which aroused my curiosity. "It is a Siva mala," he explained. "The beads are seeds from a tree and because of their peculiar shape and division into five parts, they remind one of the five faces of Lord Siva." Some new visitor had given this mala to him as a present. Suddenly he decided to give it to me. I was embarrassed. I had not asked with any such intention. But he insisted: "Take it to Canada. Start a Yoga Museum. It will be interesting to others also."

I felt terrible. He did not know what a great lesson he taught me. Besides his few pieces of cloth and some books from his Master, Ramananda possesses nothing. The mala was actually a requisite for his spiritual practice, yet he was happy to give it away. I felt ashamed. For the first time I knew how much I possessed, which I overestimate in importance. A little experience like this one can teach more than the study of all the books. Spirituality must be practiced, must be lived.

I looked at the mala. "Lord Siva," Swamiji explained, "can see with four faces to all corners of the world, and with the fifth he can see below and above. The eye of righteousness does not miss anything. His ears can listen to the four corners of the world and he can hear the inner unspoken secrets. Nothing is lost to the law of karma, neither the good nor the bad."

On the way to my kutir Swami Satchitananda passed by, his head completely shaven and his beard gone. "Do you recognize me, Mother?"

"Certainly. Why not? You have just shaved your hair all off, still I recognize you by your eyes. But why did you do it?"

"I wanted to see if I had some attachment to all this hair. Did you ever think what kinds of attachment one can have? Attachment comes very easily." Then he gave me a long discourse on this subject. Although only a young fellow of 25, he took his step to renunciation very seriously. Already he had become aware of the subtlety of spiritual temptations. God's grace will crown his efforts with success someday.

25 November

Several days ago when Gurudev came from his kutir it seemed that every Western visitor was in the group around Sivananda. The Indian lady from next door and I went to meet him. Master stopped and said in a loud, clear voice,

"I gave you some work to do and I haven't heard anything of it, and this was at least a week ago." Because I had no work, I looked at the young lady beside me. She seemed to be at a loss but Master clarified very quickly to whom he was speaking. "I thought German people were very reliable and industrious. How do you explain this?"

I had no idea what he was talking about. I searched my mind very quickly, but I could not come up with any indication and, of course, no answer to such criticism.

Master continued, "I don't understand that. You promised and I have heard nothing from you. You haven't given any indication how far advanced you were with the work." I was very tempted by now to defend myself and ask him what work he was really talking about, but I refrained from this impulse and kept silent.

In fact, I kept silent for quite a few days, but finally I found an opportunity to ask him if he had been teaching me a lesson. And if I ask for an explanation now, is it still my ego? Master seemed at first not to know what I was talking about. I went into more details.

He said he had addressed his complaints to me because in India, "We have the custom of scolding our own daughter in order to teach our daughter-in-law a lesson." I could not help feeling this was highly unjust. In fact, I was stunned. If Gurudev carefully watched my reactions I do not know. I was too absorbed in my own thoughts.

After my initial feeling of the injustice done to me in front of the Western people who were already very critical of me, I began to realize that his saying, "We scold our own daughter to teach our daughter-in-law a lesson," gave me an indication of my relationship to Gurudev. As if he wanted to make sure I understood correctly, he remarked, "It was meant for the girl who was standing next to you." Then with a warm smile, Gurudev said, "You are very close to me." I am becoming more and more acquainted with the Eastern way of thinking.

Radha performs a dance mudra for Swami Sivananda. "Learn as many mudras as you can. You will put my songs into dances."

Our play of auntie and nephew

is still going on. This morning Gurudev sent for me and when I came into his sight, he waved his hand to hurry me. Climbing up the stairs, I called, "How is my beloved nephew this morning?" At once he picked up the joke and told the new visitors that I was his auntie. They were rather puzzled and looked at him questioningly. Unaccustomed to Master's way of making fun, they did not know what to think of him. Most people, in particular Western visitors, expect him to sit all the time on a tiger skin in deep meditation or absorbed in samadhi.

Master handed me a lovely bunch of flowers saying, "They speak to you! They smile at you. Swami Swaroopananda will take you to Dehra-Dun to learn some more Indian dances." I gasped, but he continued, "Learn as many mudras as you can. You will put my songs into dances. Come back quickly. And have lunch with me today."

"But, Gurudev, I don't have any money to stay in a hotel and buy food."

"But Mrs. Radner invited you to stay in her house, so you can have a place there."

I remembered this invitation, "I am not convinced she really meant it. She might not even be in Dehra-Dun, and then what should I do?"

Gurudev said, "Let the Lord take care of everything."

I gave a big sigh. My heart was heavy. "How do I pay for my dance lessons?"

The Master said, "The Lord will take care of that, too."

I was his only guest at lunch. A table had been set near him, laden with all kinds of fruits and a big glass of pomegranate juice. Somehow he has found out that I have a great liking for this. Several other special Indian dishes were served by young *sadhaks* (novices). According to Indian custom food is taken with the right hand. I had adopted this and Gurudev seemed to like the idea that I tried to adjust myself as much as possible. At the end of the meal a small gesture showed his great humility. He held a bowl of warm water for me to wash my hands. Afterwards he took his towel and dried them.

As I went back to my kutir, I thought I don't want to go to Dehra-Dun. I don't want to learn Indian dancing. I want to stay here at the ashram near Swamiji and learn whatever I can absorb. I have become aware, by sitting literally on his doorstep and doing whatever work he gives me, of the extension of his aura around him. Most of my learning is by listening to what Gurudev says to other people, then applying it to myself — whenever I have enough awareness to see that it does apply to myself. Even if I can learn the dances in one month instead of two as he has suggested — and I can't imagine that this is possible — I'm still not willing to give up that amount of time. Again the question of obedience to the guru comes up in my mind. So when Swami Swaroopananda comes to get me, I will follow Master's wishes. I will go, but with a heavy heart.

27 November

When I arrived at the house

of Mrs. Radner, it was obvious that I was not welcome. There are people who do such things: they forget to say, "Please don't make use of my invitation because I really don't mean it." I looked at Swamiji and asked him what he could suggest. He just shrugged his shoulders and then got up and left the room. I thought he was going to the bathroom but realized after 15 minutes that he was trying to get out of this unpleasant situation. What was I to do? Where could I go? I was not financially prepared to live in a hotel.

My only hope was to wait until he returned and could take me back to the ashram.

Mrs. Radner told me that her husband was on a business trip and that she wanted to go to town. Her driver was waiting and I could go with her if I liked. I decided not to go because I hoped that Swami Swaroopananda had just left to do some shopping for the ashram and I did not want to miss him.

While Mrs. Radner was out, a German lady, Mrs. Trautmann, arrived on a bicycle. Mrs. Radner had invited her for tea. Mrs. Trautmann asked me how I came to India and where I lived. I told her my whole story and also why I had come to Dehra-Dun, that originally Mrs. Radner had invited me to stay, but I had come either at the wrong time and it did not suit her, or perhaps I had taken her invitation seriously when it was only polite conversation.

Mrs. Trautmann came like an angel to my rescue. She said that her daughter takes dance lessons; also that she would have to go to New Delhi and perhaps I could be of some service to her by staying in the house and seeing the children off to school. As we talked we found out that her daughter had the same dance master I was to go to, and he came to her house for private lessons. If I were there too, it would be more fun for both of us.

After a little while, Mrs. Radner returned from her shopping. During tea Mrs. Trautmann suggested to Mrs. Radner that I should move to her house, since her daughter had the same dance teacher and also that having me in the house would mean that she would feel easier when she went to New Delhi for a few days to be with her husband. Mrs. Radner was only too glad to get rid of me so easily. She offered her car to drive us to Mrs. Trautmann's house. When we arrived Mrs. Trautmann was joyfully greeted by her little boy of three. Her two daughters were not back from school yet. We settled down for a cup of tea the cook had prepared, and some of Mrs. Trautmann's excellent cake. We were both happy to be able to speak in our own language.

After a little while she got up and showed me the house. She also introduced me to the servants, telling them in English that they would have to obey me as I was taking her place. Finally, she gave me over 100 rupees in cash and, for some unknown reason, two blank signed checks, urging me to put them away carefully and to use them should I be in need of some extra money. She explained to me that the cook did the shopping for the food and that the sweeper must never, according to Indian tradition, touch anything in the kitchen except the floors, otherwise the cook would leave. "The Indians have so many tabus in their caste system that it makes life rather complicated, and sometimes it gets on my nerves." She feels it will take at least 500 years before there can be a change in the laws and the customs, which are so deeply ingrained in the Indians.

Then she told me that the girls would be coming home soon. She showed me to my room and, with an understanding smile, she said, "You must be very tired. Take some rest and get yourself settled."

At dinner I met the two daughters, one 18 and one 12. Our conversation centered around dance. I asked Liz if Siva or Krishna have become more than words to her through the Dance of Siva, or the Dance of Krishna.

"Oh, yes," she admitted, "I have more understanding now. The symbolic language of the mudras, the hand and finger positions, as well as the meaning of the dress and the jewels, is fascinating."

We kept on talking this way for some time and, having a common interest, became friends. Mrs. Trautmann regretted that her younger daughter did not share the same interest. She told the girls that their father had phoned from New Delhi and that she would have to leave the day after tomorrow. She stressed how wonderfully it had worked out that she had met me — I spoke German, Liz would now have a companion for the dance lessons and they would have somebody to talk to while she was absent.

While she was speaking to her children it went through my mind that Gurudev had said, "Trust the Lord." I can't say that I had trusted. My anxiety was much too great and, really, my surrender to the situation was not a choice of mine. Feelings of gratitude started to well up within me. When I took Mrs. Trautmann's hand to thank her, it took all my will power not to cry. Then I excused myself so that she could be with the family.

I have a great need at this moment to be alone and reflect on events.

28 November

When Swami Swaroopananda came back

around noon he was astonished to find out from Mrs. Radner that I had moved to Mrs. Trautmann's. I quickly scribbled a note for him to take back to Gurudev thanking him for this test of my faith.

Liz and I practiced our dancing in a spacious veranda which, like the house, was built of stone and was very cool. When the dance teacher, Mr. Devasatyam, came, his face remained expressionless when Swami Swaroopananda told him on behalf of Swami Sivananda that I was to learn six dances. It is easy to guess what was going on in his mind — that this was an impossible request. He must have accepted the job only because of the money. He got three times as much for an hour teaching foreigners as he would have got from Indians.

After he left, Liz showed me all the dances she had already learned. I suggested that during her next class I would tape the rhythm and the songs she danced to and she could put in some remarks about the movements. Then she could do the same for my class. She thought she would ask her father for a tape recorder for Christmas, knowing he would be only too happy to give her one.

After supper Mrs. Trautmann invited me into her little salon to have tea with her and a private talk. I became aware of what a wonderful lady she is, concerned that she should be a good stepmother to her husband's two girls and a good wife to him. I also got an insight into her own struggle about God. She had a very old Bible and she showed me some books that are apparently not included in what we call the Bible today, stories of healings associated with the baby Jesus. She warned me not to become too absorbed in Sivananda. "The Indians have a sort of hypnotic power," she said. "Don't forget your own heritage."

She also had an old edition of a Christian Science book and I pointed out to her some inscriptions on the front that were from the Vedas, Upanishads and other Indian scriptures. "Oh, I don't mean," she said, "that you can't let yourself be inspired." She became somewhat pensive, then she changed the subject.

"I am only too happy to pay the cost of your dance lessons because it will be so good for Liz and I am most happy to leave everything in your care." I felt grateful because I knew that I had met her by some sort of divine appointment but my attempt to thank her was feeble as I was embarrassed to talk in this way about God, or even to pronounce the word. Mrs. Trautmann did not know what to say so again she changed the subject.

Soon she excused herself to get ready, as she was leaving in the morning for New Delhi. When I retired to my room, my thoughts continued to whirl around. I had a good night's sleep. There was no problem of being up at 5 for meditation. My bedroom has its own bath, Indian style, of course. Shortly after 6 I was dressed to see Mrs. Trautmann and her little boy off. The girls still had some time left before going to school and I joined them for their breakfast. While Liz and I had quickly made friends through our common interest, I had yet to get to know the younger daughter, Uta.

Later the servant came to take the girls to school. I went into the kitchen where the cook greeted me very respectfully as the mistress and called me Memsahib, asked me if I wanted anything special for lunch and proudly told me of all the German dishes he could cook. We discussed dinner and I decided I would have tea in the late afternoon with the girls when they came home. Then I went around the house to familiarize myself with the way Mrs. Trautmann kept things in order, so I could continue in the same way and thereby fulfill her wishes. Back in my bedroom I tidied up a few more things. I wrapped up the two blank checks in a piece of old newspaper and tucked it among many other papers in my suitcase, which I could lock.

I went into the garden and sat by the pond, watching the goldfish. Then I explored the garden. There were orange trees and lemon trees. It was a strange sensation to pluck an orange from its own tree, when all my life I have only bought it in a shop. It was a sort of joyful experience. I had a tiny little compass and tried to find the best place in the garden for meditation where I could face either north or east.

When the girls came from school I chatted with them, telling them how much I liked the house, the quietness of the romantic garden and sitting by the pool watching the goldfish. Liz told me that they were happy that the monsoon was over and how hard it had rained. She said you could stand naked in the garden when the rain comes down and you could not be seen there.

Suddenly Uta joined the conversation. "You know," she said, "we always need one of the servants to take us to school now," (I had wondered about this in the morning), "because one time some young Indians threw me off my bicycle. They wanted to investigate my body. I yelled and screamed." Liz became very embarrassed and for a moment I was stunned.

Again I realized my naivete that I did not think for a moment that a country that was spreading the Divine Light would also have so many expressions of the dark. Liz tried to soften the impact by saying, "Well the Orientals are much more passionate and also curious." Then with an intense look that tried to convey something, she said, "Uta just didn't understand."

I asked them how much homework they had to do and if they had to work after supper. I invited them any time they wanted my company to let me know. Uta told me that she would rather do her homework after supper because her mother allows her to go to a nearby military camp where she rides the horses to give them their daily exercise. Liz said she did the same except on days when she had dancing classes. That was fine because it would mean for me even more peace and quiet, a luxury which I had not experienced for a long time. I felt very happy and relaxed.

4 December

I have breakfast with the girls,

but otherwise they are pretty much on their own and they are very happy about it. I find they give me no reason to reprimand them. It is an easy job.

In the afternoon when Mr. Devasatyam came, I watched how he taught Liz and I was surprised that he never demonstrates anything—everything is theoretical. He just tells Liz the posture or position and corrects it; then he gives the rhythm with two cymbals and in a monotonous voice sings the story telling what Liz is dancing. However, I also realize that all my previous lessons from Indians who had come to Germany were very amateurish. I will have to start from scratch, and how I shall learn six dances in two months (certainly not one) I do not see.

The tape recorder proves very handy because after each sequence I tell on the tape what I did. I don't think Mr. Devasatyam likes that very much. Because the dances that Liz knows are different from the ones that I have to learn, she can only be of some help to me, but even that is very much appreciated. Liz pays Mr. Devasatyam after each lesson. "That is a precaution," she said when he had left, "to make sure he will come back. You never know in India when people will keep a promise." Obviously Liz has great understanding as well as considerable talent, to learn without ever having a demonstration. Mr. Devasatyam is short and fat and probably incapable of demonstrating, but Liz told me that when there is a performance at the Art Center, the best dancers are trained by him. That is why he was chosen as her teacher.

The best time to practice is either very late at night when it is cooler, or in the early morning hours. The physical energy needed to practice Indian dances is tremendous. Every time after practicing I have to take all my clothes off—they are dripping wet, but the facilities for getting my clothes washed and dried are very good. The servant who takes the girls to school in the morning and to the riding camp is also the laundry man.

7 December

Mr. and Mrs. Trautmann came home

this afternoon and he greeted me in a very friendly way. Before taking a rest after the long drive from New Delhi he told me: "Only an hour ago, I heard of your stay. My wife suddenly started thinking that she had given house and money to a stranger and she became worried about what might have happened, so she confessed the whole thing to me."

Mrs. Trautmann blushed at her husband's words. "Please forgive me," she said apologetically, "I go by my intuition, but when my reason starts to make me think, I begin to worry. But everything is fine. After we have changed clothes we will have a nice supper together and talk."

"I have not used your checks. The cash you left was sufficient. I will get them."

"No, no, it is all right now. It can wait until tomorrow."

Liz took me aside, "You believe in the goodness of people? Our mother is too confident, one day she will pay for it."

"If we have to pay for our belief in the goodness of others, Liz, it is only a test of how strong our belief is. If it is weak, then we may stop having confidence in people or even become bitter. But if it is strong, we will go on believing in the goodness of people in spite of evidence to the contrary."

After dinner Mr. Trautmann reminded me of an old German custom, that of having a glass of red wine with a cigarette. I accepted the wine, but not the cigarette. When I began intensely practicing pranayama the habit of smoking left me. He talked of his travels about Afghanistan, where he had been first as a war prisoner, later as an engineer, and India — he seems to know every corner of it.

I decided to tell him about my dream experience of the temple built in a peculiar style with a flight of steps leading into the water, the small boat tied up ready to take me to the other shore, how at the moment I had my foot in the boat, a firm voice called me back and willingly, but with a heavy heart, I obeyed. While speaking I drew a simple sketch of this temple. Mr. Trautmann gave a short look. "That is Kashmir." He became deeply absorbed in his thoughts. No one dared to disturb the silence.

After some time Mr. Trautmann looked at his wife. "Let Radha stay here as long as she wishes. Give her all comfort. Give her the key to my bookcase." Again he became silent. Mrs. Trautmann and the two daughters looked at me curiously. I felt a bit uneasy but Mrs. Trautmann did not seem to mind that he had called me Radha instead of Mrs. Hellman. She made a sign that perhaps he would say something else of importance. She not only seemed to be accustomed to his unusual behaviour, but even to expect it.

"Swami Sivananda is your Master. Very likely it is he who will call you back to do some work. But later on you will take off to the other shore. Did he tell you when you will get Liberation? Realization?"

"No, he did not, although once he told me, no more birth for Radha."

"I would not be surprised if there had been a connection previously."

"He mentioned that I had lived and worked with him before in another lifetime and for that reason I had to come again."

"I see, I see." Mr. Trautmann had an idea for this mysterious dream. "What you perceived was memory from the past. He had called you formerly. There is a peculiar thing one has to understand. When a Guru has a mission, he comes back with all his former disciples. It will be your last time perhaps." Mr. Trautmann then recounted many of his experiences in India. We parted long after midnight.

10 December

This morning Mrs. Trautmann told me

of plans for us to go by car to Mussourie with her daughters and another lady. At the last minute Mrs. Trautmann developed a pain in her chest and decided to stay home. Mussourie is a hill station from where one can see the snow peaks of the Himalayas. The weather was clear and after a two hour walk we rested and enjoyed the view as we ate our picnic. Gigantic, wild, majestic, lay the mountain range before us. Somewhere to the north must be Kailas, the abode of Lord Siva. Gurudev has promised to take me to Kailas. Siva! Siva! When will you become a reality to me? When will you be more than just a word?

On our way to reach the car in Mussourie we were stopped by a Sikh shopkeeper. He held up a little Tibetan figure in bronze. "You must take this. You must buy this, madame. It belongs to you." I felt no inclination for the long and strenuous process of bargaining. However, I only had 15 rupees with me, so whatever price he asked, I could not pay more than that. After all, why should I buy this little bronze? I counted my money in front of him to rid myself of this situation. He could see there was 25 rupees missing from the price marked, but he gave it to me for 15, which was all I had. When we returned Mrs. Trautmann was greatly attracted to it. I was pleased to give it to her as a little present in appreciation, but something strange happened. When she took it into her hands, she immediately put it down as though it were hot. "Do you know anything about metal?"

"Not much." I took the little bronze into my hands. As I held it its weight increased. Finally I had to put it down. We looked at each other, but did not dare to speak about it.

Before retiring she brought it very, very carefully to my bedroom. "It belongs to you, Radha. You must keep it."

I do not know how long I had slept when a beautiful smell awoke me. I quickly realized that I would not be able to go back to sleep. I felt as bright and as fresh as a daisy, so I re-arranged my pillows and settled for meditation. But I felt cold and soon became aware that the coldness seemed to increase, so I pulled my blanket around me to keep me warm.

I am in the habit of starting meditation with eyes open, focusing on one spot. Across from the bed is a big window with a view to the garden. I do not close the curtains or the wooden shutters because I like to be awakened by the dawn. The wall, the window and the curtains became invisible. It was as though a cloud were forming, like fog with a luminous quality to it. Then the fog, as it moved in waves, seemed to form something like a grotto from which icicles hung. Light played on the icicles and there was a bright light in the center that fluctuated.

When it dimmed somewhat I recognized that in the center of it someone was sitting. I could clearly distinguish the outlines of a human body sitting in a perfect lotus posture. Around the head there seemed to be a fantastic headdress of such beauty it could only be a mass of jewels. After my first surprise I wanted to see the face. I was totally involved in this experience and I followed the fluctuations of the light as it would appear and disappear. He was sitting in a sea of flowers in a splendor so magnificent, that the flowers seemed to give off light, too. The face was of no particular nationality. The eyes were looking straight at me. They seemed to be at once soft and firm. The smile I can only describe as a heavenly smile. I was entranced. Then the light dimmed, all became fog and suddenly was gone.

This morning Mrs. Trautmann told me that she had come into my room in the night thinking that I had forgotten to turn off the light, but when she entered there was no electric light on. She saw me meditating and withdrew to the adjoining room, hoping that she too would be able to meditate and become aware of such light. I kept quiet about my experience. I myself have no rational explanation for it.

13 December

Mukunda is the Trautmann's sweeper.

He had been a sweeper formerly for an English family, where he picked up some English and he would often talk to me.

"Memsahib, shall I marry?"

"I don't know, Mukunda! Do you have a girl friend?"

"I know always when you meditate!" he said. "Things have changed, since you came here. How long will you stay?"

"I am supposed to learn six dances. But I have to be back as soon as possible. Definitely before Christmas."

"I am only a sweeper. I am a poor man. I will never see your guru."

"Nonsense, Mukunda. Swami Sivananda accepts all who have an earnest spiritual desire. Would you like to go and see him?"

"How can I hope for that? I cannot go and come back in one day. For a sweeper there are no holidays."

"I will ask Mrs. Trautmann if she will let you go for the weekend. But you must promise to return Monday night. I will pay your fare."

Mukunda could not say anything, but all day his eyes hung on my face, trying to find out whether I had spoken to Mrs. Trautmann or not. Of course she agreed. She was very much in favor of this idea. Servants who have a spiritual interest are more trustworthy. He was extremely happy and I wrote a note for him to hand to Swami Chidananda so that he could give it to Gurudev at night in satsang.

16 December

Mukunda returned this morning

with a note from Swami Chidananda. When he thanked me he said, "Your Master is surely a great one. How great I don't know. But I do know, he is a very kind one."

In Mr. Trautmann's library was a German edition of the New Testament and I felt inspired to read it. I have not looked at the Bible for ten years. I opened it at Matthew 18:10.

See to it that you do not treat one of these little ones with contempt; I tell you, they have angels of their own in heaven that behold the face of my heavenly father continually.

God's ways are very mysterious. I felt like spending some time in prayer.

17 *December*

Mrs. Trautmann left today

to follow her husband to New Delhi. After she had gone I sat by the pond, my favorite place for doing japa or meditation. For two or three malas I had recited my mantra, but my concentration was poor because my stomach was upset. Suddenly three old men appeared, one with white hair and beard, one with no hair at all but with glasses, and the little old saint from Vasistha Guha, each with his mala. Silently I saluted them. There was no word. They had come to support me in my efforts. I didn't enquire who the other two were, I just accepted the experience with a deep feeling of gratitude. I had had little inclination to do my set number of malas, but in their company I completed it. Then they vanished in the same manner as they had come.

Radha with Mr. Devasatyam, the dance instructor. ". . .it is a miracle to me how you learn these dances so fast."

Yesterday I had my first lesson

of the Siva dance. I was in a high mood, in spite of the strain caused by the intricacies of this dance and my upset stomach. (My whole intestinal system is in pain and the increasing cramps made me fearful of eating anything this last week). Somehow my good spirits affected my dance teacher too. For the first time, as he directed me through the complete dance, he was carried away. He told me some other inspiring stories of Lord Siva.

"I did not believe in gurus, Mrs. Hellman. I am brought up in the Christian faith, but your guru, I don't know. Anyway, it is a miracle to me how you learn these dances so fast."

"Come and meet him. Shall I get an invitation for you?"

"Yes, but when I come, I will come with my wife and my little son. Can we stay overnight? Will we get food?"

"Everything, everything. Nothing to worry about. Yes, he is a wonderful master — kind, generous, helpful. All are welcome to him." I felt I was overflowing with thanks for Gurudev.

Mr. Devasatyam suggested teaching Liz and me the Radha-Krishna dance. I thought this was a splendid idea and suggested to Liz that she come at Christmas to the ashram when her family will be in New Delhi and we will perform the dance as a gift for Master. Mr. Devasatyam also offered to teach us the Siva-Parvati dance.

After the class I felt quite ill. I was very depressed, realizing that I am getting worse with each day — fearful of eating food, yet hungry. My weakness is increasing.

Yesterday Liz took the dance class alone.
I just couldn't, I was too weak. In the afternoon Uta announced that a *sadhu* had come by car and wanted to see me. I was puzzled, *sadhus* don't use cars. Perhaps someone had given a swami a lift and he had come to meet me.

On the terrace I met Swami Venkatesananda. I called out his name joyfully, when Chidanandaji emerged from the car and also Swami Satchitananda. He put his finger on his lips and pointed secretively to the car. I dragged myself over. Master sat inside! I laid my head and hands in his lap. "Gurudev!"

As he made no effort to come out, I urged him: "Will you not come into the house and bless it?"

He did not refuse. He had hardly entered the room when he saw my hot water bottle in the chair.

"Who is sick?" He looked at me. I couldn't hide my weakness.

At this moment Mr. and Mrs. Trautmann returned from New Delhi. They were happily surprised to find their visitors. Mrs. Trautmann immediately ordered some tea, biscuits and chocolates. Master and his three disciples in their bright orange robes, the family and I, we formed a big circle. Master remembered, after he had enquired about the Trautmann's trip, that I was sick. He put his hand in his pocket and, like a little boy, pulled out a handful of crumbs, shreds of chocolate, broken pieces of nuts, ends of string, bits of fluff, and stretching his hand out to me, he said, "Here is your medicine." I took the handful, picked out one piece of nut and ate it, and knew I would be all right. My mind flashed back to the dirty milk cups at the ashram. I had been so critical of Gurudev for allowing such unsanitary conditions. Suddenly I understood that nourishment from the Master has a quality far above cleanliness.

Mrs. Trautmann looked at me very intently. She seemed to be

trying to express something, which she wanted me to convey to the Master. She did not want to speak German out of politeness and I am not a mind reader, but sometimes people can project their thoughts.

I suggested that we have Master's kirtan and prayers. Mrs. Trautmann gave me a brief nod. With a sweet smile Gurudev agreed and began at once. He likes to sing the Lord's name and inspire others to do the same. The children joined in, the parents listened with closed eyes — in particular, Mr. Trautmann seemed to be far away. A long period of silence followed the prayers and then Master blessed everyone. When he called Liz's name and mine together, she came from behind and put her arms around me. "Stick to her," Master said to Liz.

"I like Radha very much. I will keep in touch with her by letter."

"Visit her in the ashram." Master looked around. "You all should come, the whole family. Be my guests. Let us see your dances." With that Gurudev got up. Everybody was very, very happy. We all accompanied Master to the car and we followed with our eyes till it disappeared.

When we returned to the house Mrs. Trautmann hugged me tenderly. "I am very grateful, Radha, because of you we had the Master's visit. Perhaps he knew you were sick and needed his help."

"He would have come just the same, without my being here. You don't know how wonderful he is. His motto is, bring the Divine Light to every house."

Mr. Trautmann said to me, "Previously I had no desire to meet him, although I had heard of him, because there were things which irritated me. But I see that one must get one's opinion by personal contact. I liked him and his way very much. These men around him gave me a very fine impression. It takes a great character to form such characters."

22 December

This morning we had breakfast
all together and I enjoyed it very much, having my first real meal
in nearly two weeks. Mrs. Trautmann was horrified. What I
thought was a cold in the intestines, she gave the real name of dys-
entry and wanted me to take a special diet and have the doctor
come. I waved that off." Master gave me medicine. Didn't you
hear it?"

"It is your faith in him, Radha. But I don't believe that can heal
infections. When do you return?"

"Master wanted me to come on Wednesday, but I can get a lift
with the Radners on Thursday. Because of the tape recorder it will
be more practical to accept that."

"Would you like to make him a Christmas cake? Then just go
ahead." I spent the rest of the afternoon happily in the kitchen.

I have enjoyed my month here — it has given me a chance to
get a perspective on the period at the ashram — to validate my
experiences, proving they were not just the magic of the aura of
Sivananda.

23 December

I am so happy to be back.
Guy Lafond, my concert pianist from Canada, who has been
travelling in Europe, has come to the ashram and greeted me
when I arrived. Highly sensitive and with no instrument to
express his feelings, he longed to share his thoughts. We talked
about the different approaches on the spiritual path, the many
possible concepts, the differences in the schools of philosophical
thought, all this play with words. It has made him confused as I
was myself.

Then the differences between East and West are so hard to understand. In Germany everything is organized to the very dot, everybody has enough to eat, everybody has a roof over his head and still there is so much unhappiness and frustration and the percentage of mentally disturbed people is frighteningly high. Here there is no comfort, everywhere dirt and disease, and hardly anybody is mentally disturbed. At home the majority of people is honest and if there is crime, it is big crime; here there is no big crime, but the small crimes occur so frequently that every city looks like a big prison, all houses are surrounded by walls and the shops have to have barred windows and doors. And yet in this place are found spiritual giants. "Crazy! Crazy!" No wonder Guy was somewhat confused. On top of this, the ashram here is just the very opposite from what he had expected, knowing the orderliness and discipline of Catholic monasteries from personal experience.

"Preconceived ideas, Guy!" I told him. "Shake them off. Be free. Don't draw conclusions. Certain things exist only under certain conditions, come alive only under certain conditions. We have to accept this. Give yourself time for development, for understanding. Consider also that we have indulged in oversimplifications. Our senses are the organs of our perceptions. You might enjoy making experiments to find out how much you can depend on them, how accurate they really are. It will give you some fun to find out how your mind works."

"Who are you, Mrs. Hellman?" We both laughed.

"Your own Self!" I echoed Sivananda. "And you must tell me not 'who' you are but 'what' you are!"

"You are already Indianized. Have you heard of the bhang or pang leaf, to induce a state of awareness by inhalation, or something like that?"

"Yes, I have. But there is no shortcut. Sorry. Neither bhang nor pang will remove egos. You experience a different state of mind, a different sensation, but you still don't know any more than before."

He sighed, "I came for a guru. I don't know if he is my guru."

"Why don't you ask him?"

"It must come from him. He must recognize me and inform me."

24 December

This is the 24th of December

and Swami Sivananda has ordered a long table to be put in front of his office with chairs for all Western visitors. Tea and coffee were served and that was the moment to bring out my Christmas cake. I asked one swami to get me a knife. The cake was cut already, but I needed it to lift the pieces without damaging the icing. I don't know what he thought I wanted, but in any case he never came back.

Gurudev decided to act. He took the pieces with his hands, dropped a piece on each plate and in no time was beautifully smeared with chocolate. It was really a divine comedy. We all roared with laughter, and so did Master. He is by no means a sad saint. Pictures were taken so that all guests may have a souvenir, reminding them that they have been for a little while in a paradise on earth.

Gurudev made a short Christmas speech, and then mentioned that he expected the Westerners to sing Christmas carols during the holy night. We all made long faces because nobody really knew a complete song. The old lady from Switzerland was the best. She dragged the rest of us along.

We all came as usual to satsang, and found the hall beautifully decorated with a Christ Altar, a tree resembling a Christmas tree and many, many oil lamps and candles. The atmosphere was simply wonderful. Master, in a high mood, made another short speech on the life of Christ. I regretted very much that I had not

Dancing at the ashram Christmas celebration.
"Tonight I want as your gift. . .Siva's Dance of Bliss."

Radha hides from Lord Krishna behind the veil of Maya. "No one, not even an Indian, could learn six intricate Indian dances in a month. It all comes back by memory."

brought the tape recorder. In a few simple words, Master spoke of the birth of Christ and His mission. It is Gurudev's special gift to express his profound Truth in simple words, understandable to everyone. But he surprised us a few minutes later when many parcels were carried into the hall and he started to give presents right and left.

He presented to everyone a cake, beautifully decorated with flowers and the name of the receiver. The doctor of law and the doctor of philosophy, at other times discussing Vedanta very seriously, became suddenly like children and happily carried gifts to their kutirs. The closing kirtans were sung in the name of Jesus and the Virgin Mother. Master's voice carried everybody into a high mood of joy and love. One big happy family, with children from all over the world, from many nations, celebrated a wonderful Christmas arranged by an Indian saint, Swami Sivananda.

Suddenly Master addressed me and asked me where his Christmas present was. I was embarrassed and said, "I have given you all I have."

Gurudev said, "No, you have not."

I could not think of anything and became very unhappy. Was there anything that I had that Master had expressed a wish that I should give to him, for himself or somebody else? I could not figure out what this could possibly be. Finally he came to my rescue and said, "You learned six dances and tonight I want as your gift . . .Siva's Dance of Bliss."

One part of me was relieved and one part of me was worried because I felt I needed more practice. Mr. Devasatyam had promised to come to the ashram and orchestrate the music with the ashram musicians. However, it turned out that one of Master's devotees could sing this particular story of Siva's Dance of Bliss. Again I could not refuse Master's wish. I performed the dance and, to my amazement, faultlessly.

Gurudev's old friend and legal advisor, the retired judge, Gauri Prasad, got very excited and gesticulated, saying, "My God, is this woman talented!"

Radha and Elizabeth Trautmann perform the Radha-Krishna dance,
symbolic of the union of individual consciousness
with Cosmic Consciousness.

But Gurudev waved this aside and said, "It has nothing to do with talent. No one, not even an Indian, could learn six intricate Indian dances in a month. Did you see, she played every movement absolutely accurately? It all comes back by memory."

25 December

Christmas Day.

Boat kirtan and Ganges worship! Unforgettable! One group sang holy songs in the boat, the other on the banks of the Ganges. The voices vibrated beautifully over the water. The praise and glory of the Lord chanted or sung is a unique experience. In particular in such an atmosphere, everything seems to become holy. Music is an international language, a language that can speak to everyone's heart.

Here in the tropics after sunset, darkness comes very fast, before one realizes it is there. As soon as it was dark the Indian ashramites on the shore lit many, many oil lamps. Slowly, one by one, they were placed on the water, and flowers were thrown into the Ganges. Flowers and the burning lamps floated gently down the holy river. Some singers went into a divine ecstasy.

I felt the Master's eyes on me. As I looked up to him, an indescribably soft smile greeted me. A young Indian mother placed her baby in my arms; she put her kashmir shawl over me to keep me warm. (A tender gesture of her sympathy. I did not feel cool.) Again I looked at Sivananda.

"Love is the language of the heart. Love finds always a way to express itself. Love unites people!"

This satsang many pairs of eyes greeted the Master through a veil of tears. How many has he inspired to turn to a divine life? To turn the mind to God?

Liz has come to the ashram

and we both went to Master's kutir to discuss with him dance performances between Christmas and New Year's. As always, swamis were coming and going with letters and papers for him to sign. While he was busy with this, Liz admired a gold locket I wore, which was an old family piece from my great-grandmother. It could be opened and there was a picture of Gurudev on the inside. Master glanced up at that moment and said to me, "Why don't you give it to her? This is the best way to renounce. If you give things to people which they greatly admire, then you will not regret that you gave them away. Renunciation is necessary to overcome attachment."

I was surprised because he had assured me that I was not one of the four to be initiated into *Sannyasa* and yet this sounded as though he were trying to prepare me for renunciation. My thoughts were interrupted by the further discussion that Liz and I should do the Radha-Krishna dance together. We decided that, as I am a couple of inches taller, I would dance the part of Krishna and she would dance the Radha part. Gurudev wants to have the dance filmed, so it will be done in the outer courtyard of the temple.

Then a young man came in and spoke to Gurudev, who went outside. We followed and found that the architect's wife, who was one of the Western visitors, had taken many of her belongings, put them in a pile and then asked one of the young *sadhus* to get her a box of matches. She was going to renounce all her possessions. The young *sadhu* had enough sense to go and get Gurudev. She was just beaming.

He looked over all the things that she was going to renounce and picked up a few pieces of costume jewelry and handed them to people in the crowd that was gathering around. Then he gave a pair of earrings to an Indian girl, saying they would look very nice

Radha showing her golden locket as Swami Venkatesananda looks on.
"If you give things to people which they greatly admire,
then you will not regret that you gave them away."

on her. He said that since Mrs. Stein was taking the path of renunciation, instead of burning and destroying all these things, it would be so much better to give them to people who would appreciate each item. Mrs. Stein didn't seem at all pleased but he took no notice of her expression and gave everything away to the ever-increasing number of people in the group.

He said, "You see, no matches are needed and how happy you have made so many people by your act of renunciation!"

As she was wearing a great deal of makeup, Gurudev suggested that she go to the Ganges, take a bath and come back looking as natural as possible, and then put on one of the nice saris she had bought for herself. She was furious. In order to prevent her from asking for things back from people, Gurudev said, "What is given is given." He also said that by her renunciation she had collected a great deal of good karma for herself.

As she always wore a huge hat with a veil, Gurudev suggested that she remove this "veil of maya." His last dramatic demand was that she should go back to Europe by herself and leave her son in his care. This was too much. She lost all her self-control and in a great outburst of anger she shouted at him, "Never, in this filthy, dirty place where people have no manners! I will never leave my son here!"

Gurudev just walked calmly away.

29 December

Swami Nadabrahmananda

has not only taught me bhajans and kirtans, but he has become my music guru in a true sense. My interest in devotional music has increased in proportion to my understanding that without devotion the struggle on the spiritual path is a hundred times harder. Master himself often warns us that without devotion, reasoning power will give tremendous knowledge with one hand and very likely as much vanity with the other.

Musical practice has increased to four and five hours a day. I do not get tired of it and satsang is no more something I avoid or regret because of loss of sleep, but most nights I feel an expanding awareness of the power of sound and its effect on the mind, the body, the nerves, the feelings. I have begun to realize the importance of sound in our everyday life. Music stimulates our moods and feelings. The sound of our voice provides an interpretation of our words. Qualities of voice influence our judgment of friends, or people in general, more than we think.

2 January 1956

Mr. Devasatyam came yesterday

to give me, in cooperation with the ashram musicians, the orchestration for the dances he has taught me. We spent all night. The swamis involved did their very best. It was really touching. Tired and exhausted, but still with a sweet smile, they departed: "Nothing to thank, Mataji. If we could be of some service to you, we are happy."

Young Satchitanandaji said, "You cannot forget me. You have taken my voice and, when you play your tape, you will have to remember me. You cannot forget me anymore, Mother."

"No, I cannot, even without your voice. Who could forget all this wonderful love? God has shown me His love through you."

Usually Master goes first

to Venkatesananda's kutir to sign letters and to check through certain mail, so I sat on the steps and waited for him. When he came he called me to follow him in and offered me a seat opposite his own. "You want to stay here?" he asked me.

"Yes, very much, if I may!"

Long pause.

"Go back. I will print a pamphlet for you that will help you."

"Gurudev, I don't think I can do that. I am afraid I could never take a small percentage of all the criticism that you have to stand. I could not live a life like you. I am not afraid that money or admiration would go to my head. I had both during the years of my career. The time is over when I put a value on things like that. But I cannot tolerate jealousy and hypocrisy. I could not live a life according to the imagination of other people. And first and last of all, I have not got the purity of mind and heart to do such work."

"Purity will come by selfless service. Selfless service will make you divine. It is God's work. You are just giving Him a hand by becoming His servant."

Long silence.

"You want to have God-realization?" Master continued, "You cannot expect that without giving also. Renunciation is not renouncing your belongings, renunciation is so much more; it is your ideas, your concepts. If He gives you work, He will give the tools also." With that he got up and left for the office. Silently I followed him. My heart felt as heavy as a rock.

He turned back to me. "You must not be afraid," he said, "I promise, I will be ever with you. If you turn to your right—I will be on your right side. If you turn to the left—I will be on your left. But go ahead because I will be right in front of you. We have lived and worked together in previous births. Never forget that."

16 January

This morning Gurudev asked me,

"Have you collected all your belongings?"

"I have not started packing yet!" I answered. It was obvious that I had not listened properly. Without correcting me, he just repeated: "Have you collected your belongings?"

I was perplexed. Belongings? That is something which belongs to me and collecting means that somewhere there is something I have not yet gathered. Actually very simple, yet I had no idea what things he meant. Carefully, not to show my ignorance I asked: "How many?"

"Three," was the Master's straight answer.

Three things belong to me which I have not yet collected. Where would I have to collect them? It dawned on me that they could only be spiritual things. I ran to Swami Chidananda.

"Swamiji, how many belongings do you have?"

"I have no belongings, Mataji. I am a monk, you know that."

"But even so, to a *sannyasin* belong certain things, what are they?"

"Besides his robes, a *sannyasin* has nothing but his begging bowl, and a *kamandalu* (water pot)."

"That is only two, what is the third?"

"It happens that a master gives his disciple a tigerskin, cheeta, or deer skin! Otherwise I don't know what belongings you mean."

"Thanks, thanks, that is all I wanted to know. You have answered my question."

17 January

Today Master gave me the tigerskin.

It was brought by Mr. Jha who wanted no money for it, even though he had given 100 rupees for it to a swami who wanted to go on a pilgrimage.

It was a very strange experience. First I carried it up to my kutir and spread it on my bed. Then I decided I would take it down again to Gurudev and ask him to have the first meditation on it with me. He agreed to my request. This was the second time I had the privilege of meditating with him alone. "The skin should be carefully tanned again and then lined up," he suggested, "and you should also sleep on the skin."

Later Mr. Jha told me such a skin is very powerful. A man-eating tiger that has killed a human being is shot and the skin is later presented to a powerful yogi to convert the vibrations into *sattvic* vibrations. It will keep all the electricity you develop during meditation and preserve the magnetism which would otherwise flow into the earth. Often a guru will offer a seat on the tigerskin to devotees who wish to have children. If the creative force is not properly controlled, one should not use a tigerskin for meditation or other spiritual practice because it will increase that energy.

What will come next?—the begging bowl or the *kamandalu*?

20 January

With my hands full of new books

I stood outside Master's office. He was only a few steps from me with a group of people. Suddenly he called my name:

"Radha! Let - it - drop!"

It appeared to me that he was looking at my left hand. For a moment I hesitated, but then dropped all the books I held in that hand. But he repeated:

"Radha! Let - it - drop!"

It flashed through my mind. IT — the EGO! Not the books.

I walked over to him and touched his feet — for the first time.

Tonight in satsang I found a new arrangement. Next to Gurudev's seat was a big cushion and he invited me to sit on it. He asked me to cover my head and face. Something very strange happened. Some sort of picture seemed to impose itself on me—a river. The Ganges? I could not make it out. The flow of the water became dominant. People, houses, bushes, trees, all seemed to float in it, with it. A flow of life. Inexpressible in words, yet it was very clear. I lifted my veil and looked at Swami Sivananda. His eyes were half-closed. Then he turned his head to me and a mischievous smile spread over his face.

He said, "The language of the heart does not know any misunderstanding. When there is oneness, words become unnecessary."

It was eleven at night when the Master asked me to come into his kutir. My heart was beating fast. What would happen?

"When you go back to the West," he said, "do not work any more for money!"

"But, Gurudev, how shall I live?"

"God will look after you. Nobody else than God has looked after you till now!"

"America and Canada are very money conscious. Nobody would understand, if I start living on alms."

"Why, you are afraid! When you came to India, were you not afraid of tigers, cobras, cheetas? God has protected you here. He will protect you anywhere."

Master could not see *my* point. I made another attempt. "There are very few people who are really interested in yoga and Vedanta. If they have to look after me, I will soon be a great burden to them. And I am healthy, why should I not work?"

"Because," Master interrupted my word flow, "you cannot tell people to live on *faith* in God alone, if you don't do it yourself. You must try to be in every way an example."

How right he is! Because he himself is such an example, he has conquered my heart and convinced my mind. But I? I have not the courage to make such an experiment.

"Radha! There is still too much pride — hidden!" He hit the sore spot. No use in arguing. He is perfectly right. How can I ever hope to get out of this whole thing?

25 January

Sivananda has a certain method

of making one feel that he is concerned, that he wants to help, that he cares, and he will express it through the tangible gifts. He will also suddenly decide to stop and take a situation in hand.

Some Western visitors were very jealous of the many things that I had been given by him and one woman in the group said, "He is supposed to be a great guru but just look at this girl here, Radha. He almost heaps her with presents. Barely a day passes when she doesn't get something from him." I overheard the remarks and she is right.

Sivananda also caught her words. He then turned around and said, "Is Radha here?"

"Yes, Gurudev." I came forward and he looked at me and said, "I've given you many presents. But really these are only trinkets. They have no value because you have given me your life. There is nothing in the world that I could give you in return for what you have offered to me."

Radha performing Pada Puja for the guru. "Without thought I did all the actions that Venkatesananda whispered to me and yet everything seemed to vibrate in my whole body."

Swami Sivananda initiates Radha into the holy order of Sannyasa.
"Put your hand on the handle. Repeat what I say."

My enquiry if I could perform

Pada Puja was answered in the affirmative. Swami Paramananda agreed that there would be no visitors and Venkatesananda offered his assistance for the *Puja*. I feel so elated. I wonder if one feels like this in a state of egolessness. Paramamanda got all the garlands, flowers, fruits, milk and sweets that are needed. I feel as if all these things are my greatest treasures.

When I laid the flower garland around Master's neck, something indescribable came over me. The expression of his eyes was strange to me. But strange also were the feelings that welled up within me. Without thought I did all the actions that Venkatesananda whispered to me and yet everything seemed to vibrate in my whole body. My hands became shaky when I laid the flowers on his feet and poured the milk. I felt I knew how one would feel if one could sit at the feet of Christ, as His disciples did, and as the sinful woman did when she washed Christ's feet and dried them with her hair. Nothing can serve as a better symbol than a flower to express the devotion one feels.

When the actual *Puja* was over, Master put two *kamandalus* in front of me.

"Take yours!"

"I don't know, Gurudev!"

"Look closely."

"I don't know." I was distressed. I cannot exercise insight when I want to. Whatever was to come to me had to come by itself. If and how it could be done at will, I have not the slightest idea. Master finally picked up one and I held my hands ready to receive it, when he commanded me:

"Put your hand on the handle. Repeat what I say."

Like a little school girl I repeated his words, not knowing what it was all about. Something happened. Where was I?

Venkatesanandaji came and put his arms around me. "I must congratulate you. Now you are a *sannyasi*."

His and all the other voices seemed to be far away. I heard Master order Venkatesananda to take me to his kutir so that I could rest and he could write out the mantras and tell me all that I needed to know.

3 February

*A*s the day passed the impact of my initiation seemed to deepen, and I felt the need to retire to meditate on the meaning of the new life that I had just been plunged into. Near the ashram lie the ruins of an old temple that are invisible from the road. How I found my way there I do not know, but as I was wandering around amid the tumbled-down stones I felt an overpowering sense of familiarity about the place. I believe that I must have had some contact with this spot at some time. One tower of the original building has fallen over without being totally demolished, and there, half-buried in the sand, its arch forms a little cave-like shelter. I sat down inside and began to meditate, when I suddenly became aware that there was someone nearby.

I looked up. It was an Indian. I was not in the mood to answer the usual questions, "Where do you come from? Do you like India?" He radiated great dignity and presence and in a flash I knew this was Babaji.* I can't remember what we talked about, but suddenly he cried, "Tiger!" Terrified, I froze, holding my breath, every muscle tensed, my senses keyed to their utmost. Babaji then told me to relax. There was no tiger. He explained that he had used this means to show me that when one's concentration is at its highest one does two things—tenses the muscles and holds the breath. This state he had just produced in me by fear, but the same condition could be produced voluntarily, and used for a specific purpose.

He then went on first to illustrate and then to explain the Divine Light Invocation. He taught me the mantra for this practice in both Sanskrit and English, but I remember it only in English. I then followed his instructions and did the Invocation myself. He explained to me the technique for sharing the light with another person. He asked me to name someone for this purpose. By this time I was so shaken by all that had happened that I could not think of a single name! He suggested imagining just the outline of a human figure.

The very first time I performed the Light Invocation I could see very clearly the Light flowing into me while my eyes were closed. Babaji explained that I should practice this Invocation in order to help others and also to break the habit of thinking of myself either as the mind or as the body. The Light would help me to do so. He further told me that I should teach this to others. Then we fell silent. When I opened my eyes Babaji was gone. The sight of the Himalayas was dazzling — the same Light that I had seen flowing through my own body was streaming forth from the living rock of the mountains.

When I beheld this awe-inspiring vista my consciousness was suddenly swept up as if by an enormous, overpowering wave to a plane far beyond anything that I had ever experienced. Words could never describe this state of consciousness.

* * * * *

Editor's Note: Literally translated, Babaji means *revered father*, and is a common title for many noted teachers in India. The legendary *Mahavatar* and great guru, Babaji, as referred to here, is a figure known specifically in the Northern Himalayan region, whose mission is to undertake, in apparent and humble obscurity, the work of guiding disciples to assist in mankind's evolutionary progress. This "deathless guru" has appeared throughout the centuries in slightly different forms to various disciples. For a more complete description, see Yogananda's *Autobiography of a Yogi*, Chapter 33.

Swami Sivananda Radha at the temple site where she had received the Divine Light Invocation. "Words could never describe this state of consciousness."

I owe my knowledge of what happened next to Mr. Jitendra Nath Khuller. He was a young Indian intellectual who had been sent by his family to stay at Sivananda Ashram in the hope that it would be good for his soul. He himself was a thorough modernist and, because of his indifference, bordering on contempt, for the traditional religious and moral practices, he had been a great trial to his parents. To avoid a family crisis he had come, determined to put in his time as painlessly as possible and then to return to the life that he had mapped out for himself.

On this particular day he had gone into the town of Rishikesh to visit friends. They had just sat down to tea when he felt an unaccountable impulse to go outside. Impolite as it was, he excused himself and left. He later gave me a vivid description of how he had found me staggering along the road, looking for all the world as if I were drunk. He approached and heard me chanting *Om* and talking about the Divine Light. It was obvious that I would need help to get back to the ashram, and so he took charge just as I was starting to cross one of the bridges.

Here is inserted a report written by Jitendra, which Swami Chidananda subsequently asked for. This shows the outward events of which I have no knowledge, but which he witnessed.

* * * * *

MY EXPERIENCE WITH MOTHER RADHA
By Jitendra Nath Khuller, M.A.B.T.

That remains the most unforgettable day in my life. It was the second of February, 1956. I had been at the Lotus Feet of Sri Gurudev for the last 5 months, enjoying his grace. That day I had gone to Vishwanath Garden about three miles away from the Ashram. I had to discuss some topics on Bhakta Yoga with Swami Ramprem. I got there very late. It was about 7 p.m. when I started from that place and it was quite dark. On the way Dr. Fakkey called me and invited me to a cup of tea. I had taken a few sips at my cup when I felt a strange sensation. Perhaps it was the feeling that I was getting late for the Satsang. Yes, perhaps it was. I had not the guts to sit there any longer. I was being pulled by something and had to leave tea and depart from my friend abruptly. I was in a hurry as I had to reach the Ashram in time to be able to continue my talk on the "Upanishad."

Chandar Bhaga is a small stream just outside the town of Rishikesh. While crossing the bridge of Chandra Bhaga I noted a moving figure ahead. There was not sufficient light to see who the person was. I noted that the person was swaying and staggering. I thought it must be somebody who was drunk and quickened my pace with the thought that I might be of some help to the person, if he or she was really drunk.

When I reached the figure I heard a strange strain. It was a music floating on the wings of air, a sublime melody. I recognized the tune of that song. It was Mother Radha singing OM OM OM, HARI OM. Now I was by her side. She was not her own self. Her face had a very pale look. Her eyes seemed to be glazed, her limbs were limp and she was swaying like a plant in a storm.

"Are you alright, Mother?" I asked. But there was no reply. Just that OM OM HARI OM!

I thought she was meditating while walking and that she might need me by her side in that state. So I began to walk just behind her. There was no traffic on the road at this time. It was getting darker and colder. We passed the Andhra Ashram and were now nearing another bridge. This bridge had no protective railings. I noted that Mother Radha was not seeing anything. Mataji seemed to be walking in sleep. It seemed that she would run into bushes on the roadside. When we reached the bridge I was afraid she might fall off. I caught her hand and led her across . . .her hand. . .oh. . .it was hot . . .very hot. . . I had never seen a man with that much temperature and still breathing. It was difficult to hold on to her arm.

We crossed the bridge. In the meantime I tried many times to wake her up from that semi-unconscious state. But later on I realized that I was a fool to do so. However, she continued to walk as if she was in a daze. Then suddenly she became silent. She began to stagger dangerously. I again caught her hand, now her body was not so hot — she was going off her balance. I was at a loss what to do. Then suddenly she collapsed. She was lying near the wall just opposite the Kailas Ashram. She lay like a heap of earth. Huddled together and limp. I was at my wits end.

I recalled that little knowledge of first aid I had acquired during my schooling. I felt her pulse. It was weak and slow. I tried to feel her breath, it was not perceptible. It was not possible for me to carry her to the Ashram. Neither could I leave her in that condition and run to bring some help. Moreover, I was afraid of the snakes and scorpions which infested that area. I could not leave her there alone, to be bitten by these. I rubbed her palms. At the same time I called into her ears: "Mother wake up. It is dark and cold. There are snakes and scorpions. Wake up!"

I repeated that many times and at last there was some movement. She opened her eyes to close them again. I helped her to sit. Warmth of her body was coming back. I took off my coat and put it on to her shoulders. After about five minutes I supported her to stand on her feet.

I said, "Let us move now, Mother. Gurudev will be waiting for us."

"Gurudev," she exclaimed. "LIGHT. . .I will. . .there. . .yes . . . THE LIGHT. . . I MUST. . ."

Many words were coming out of her mouth and I could make no meaning of these. I was supporting her in my arms and pushed to make her walk. I kept supporting her and she walked. Her eyes were fixed up in the northern sky.

"Are you all right, Mataji?" I asked again.

"What do you mean," she rebuked me. "I am SATCHIT-ANANDA. I am PARAMANAND!"

I was still doubtful about her physical condition. I knew she was in a different mental plane. I asked, "Do you recognize me, Mother? Do you know who I am?"

I noted a smile spreading on her lips. She said in a whisper, "Yes, I know you! But you do not know your own SELF."

I was taken aback. In utter amazement I looked at her. Her face was now bright. It was actually luminous in the dark. Her eyes were still fixed in the northern skies. Then suddenly she cried, "The LIGHT. Don't you see it? There again. High up. . .the LIGHT."

"I cannot see it, Mataji," I said. But she made no response and we continued walking, I still supporting her.

Then she stopped.

"LIGHT! See it Jitendra. . .there."

I looked up where she was pointing. There was nothing but the darkness of the night. Little stars were trying to pierce it with their feeble rays. There was nothing unusual or abnormal. Then happened the strangest thing in my life. I felt a sensation as if some current was flowing into my body through my arms. A strange current was running into my body from Mother Radha. I felt as if I was slipping into sleep and I felt to be rising like a cloud out of my body. . .and then I saw IT! IT WAS THERE! LIGHT in the northern sky. . .bliss giving. . .shooting. . .bluish white. . . penetrating. . .strong. . .well I cannot explain it. It is impossible to do so. I do not remember what happened next. I heard words of

Mataji ringing in my ears like: light, Gurudev, and my name, in an indescribable expression.

We were walking on the secluded road. We had reached the Ashram. It was about 9 p.m. Mother seemed to be normal. In a roundabout way I told her what had happened. She remembered nothing but my reference to snakes and scorpions.

She seemed to be weak. I left her in her room and ran to the kitchen to bring some coffee or tea. I got some tea prepared and brought it back hurriedly. When I entered the room I again found Mother in a trance. I don't know if I committed a mistake by bringing her back to consciousness and making her take her tea.

Then I felt relieved. I went to satsang. I was afraid that Swamiji would ask me why I was late for my talk. But when I entered the hall, I saw his eyes fixed at the door as if waiting for me. He saw me and smiled. I felt as if he was asking me silently, "Alone?"

I replied aloud, "Yes, Swamiji. Mother Radha is now in her room."

All present laughed. To them it appeared that I had said something in reply to no question at all. Gurudev asked me aloud, in a teasing way, "Why, you are late today?"

I was going to offer some explanation, when he added, "Yes, but you have not wasted your time."

It was then that I felt certain that Gurudev knew everything. That he had used me as an instrument to protect Mataji. It was he who had blessed me to be a witness to the divine experience of Mother Radha and to be a partner also. Being a young Indian of the present generation, I had stubbornly refused to accept anything like that. Now my belief was confirmed half an hour later at the close of satsang. We were going along with Swamiji to see him off to his kutir. Mother Radha met us on the way. The Master and Mother looked at each other for a minute without words, they had their own way of communication. Then the Master's eyes turned on me for a long time, after which he nodded his head and . . .smiled.

Only the next morning I realized the greatness of that experience and still in the state of the blissful feeling had the urge to share it with others. Swami Venkatesanada was not surprised. He had seen Mother in a trance-like state, but had not realized the depth of it. His concentration had been on some important work for the Master. Swami Chidananda listened carefully, then he said, "Mataji must have been for many hours in that state. Just now Swami Nityananda was here, very excited. He had met her down in Rishikesh about lunch time. She suddenly entered his room, he was there for a few days.

"Mataji entered singing HARI OM, then sat down whispering a few things he could not understand, at the same time tears were pouring down her face. She gave him such a shock that he felt he was paralyzed. Without any word to him she left after her tears stopped. Swami Nityanandaji felt also very relieved then. He came to enquire. He realized that he should have followed to protect her.

"But Master chose you, Jitendra." I informed Chidanandaji that Swami Venkatesananda told me that Mother had had her first Puja with the Master.

"There is something very peculiar between Mother and Gurudev. We observed this from the very beginning. Perhaps the impact of remembrance was so great by the power of Sri Gurudev. Remembrance of the past."

"I always thought that the Master had his plans for her." Chidanandaji then added, "Let us be silent about it. Otherwise people will talk to her curiously and she may become embarrassed."

5 February

Yesterday morning Master asked me, "When are you going into seclusion?"

"I have been waiting for you to arrange it for me."

He made no further remark.

About five o'clock in the afternoon one of the swamis came hurriedly, "Get ready! Quick! Quick! The last boat is going in 5 minutes. I am supposed to take you across the Ganges for seclusion."

I was very glad about this news. But such a hurry? I have to prepare a few things. At least I need 15 minutes. But Swamiji thought differently, "You don't need anything. You are now a *sannyasin*. Just come."

Still I took my own blankets, soap, towels, etc. I had no idea for how long I was to stay, so I took some clothing to change. We just got in the last boat at the last minute. Swamiji carried a lantern because he would have to return in the dark on foot.

Tara was to look after my physical needs, but otherwise not to disturb my spiritual practice.

6 February

The quietness was most enjoyable. No monkeys jumping with vehemence on metal roofs to make a noise that could shake one right to the bottom of the heart. Now I could choose the hour of meditation and prayer and have a schedule I felt most beneficial. I realized the value of independence from any outward circumstances in spiritual practice, but it needs a tremendous development to be able to shut off the sense of hearing in an instant.

I woke up early this morning. It was still cold and dark. I wrapped myself up in blankets, arranged a comfortable seat on the roof and spent some time in meditation. Later on, Tara brought hot tea with bread and butter. She put everything quietly down within my reach and took her seat close by, waiting to be of some service. I felt no inclination for drinking or eating. More hours passed.

Tara had just heated the tea again and joined me at the breakfast table when visitors came. I ran up to the roof to hide myself, making Tara understand that I don't want to meet anybody. But some people can be persistent if they have set their minds on something. The gentleman and two ladies would not leave. They decided they would wait till I had finished meditation.

He spoke English and decided to look around in the house until he could talk to me. Tara made a helpless gesture when he finally stood in front of me, introducing himself as a medical doctor servicing the area beyond Lakshmanjula for the government. He invited me to lunch at his house. For the next hour I tried very hard to make him understand that I had come for seclusion, that I now was a *sannyasi* and not interested in any social activity. He insisted that at least I should meet the two ladies who were in his company. We came down from the roof garden.

If all this life is God's play, He truly must have some fun in directing and offering me a new role. One cannot order people from a house in which one is also guest. I came to the conclusion that I must accept the lunch invitation, which would mean we would leave together and once in his place, I was free to go. While he was here, there was no hope of peace. God makes it pretty hard to concentrate on Him.

The home of this Dr. Sharma was spotlessly clean and tidy. I had not seen anything like it in India up till now. The backyard of the house had been turned into a beautiful little garden with bushes and flowers. All in all, a delightful place. The two women could not speak English, so he kept the conversation going. I was unable to make out what these women did on their own account or what they were ordered to do by him.

They behaved to me with so much respect, it made me feel uneasy. Their service during the meal did not allow me to enjoy the food because they wanted to eat only food I had taken part of, as *prasad*. He then came out with his plans. "I have heard about you. One of my students goes every night to Sivananda Ashram. I want to start an ashram myself, but I want you to be our Holy Mother. And I want. . ."

"Just a minute," I interrupted him, "first of all, I am not holy. Second, my guru has very definite plans for me and I am going to follow him; third, I am still very much in need of help myself. You should have told me what you had in mind when you came. You would have spared yourself a lot of trouble."

When he saw I had no inclination to become a holy mother of his ashram, he tried to persuade me to meet his guru. I attempted to escape by saying that I had spent all my money already and could not consider traveling. He offered to pay the fare and to furnish me with all that was needed for my comfort. He was sure that his guru would give me *samadhi* right away, because I was so saintly. Sometimes it is fun to personalize God. In this play now, He is the tempter from outside, but at the same time the protector from inside and third, He is the awakener.

I finally decided to cut the whole thing short and got up to leave. Everybody was commanded to salute me with prostrations. Dr. Sharma himself handed all the rose petals to me from the morning worship. "You will change your mind, lady." He did not want to give up, "When my guru projects himself to you, will you believe?"

"I'll cross that bridge only when I come to it." I *pranamed* and left. Tara was held back. They all talked together to her in Hindi. On the way home I felt amused about this divine comedy. If God would come to me as an angel, I would ask for a little black feather in his wings. Here in India it is all Lord Krishna's play. Krishna, the playful, the mischievous one. If He wants to play His flute, everybody has to dance. But this time I did not dance, the flute woke me up. May heaven be gracious and let me be awake all the time.

11 *February*

When I returned from seclusion,

I had a message for the Master that I had promised to deliver. I also thought if I am to run an ashram I must ask him some more questions on human sexuality, and I hoped to have an opportunity to bring up this rather delicate subject. The thought that Gurudev was a medical doctor was very helpful because I did not really know how to talk about it. When I arrived at the office there was, by coincidence (or was it Gurudev's doing?) a swami who I knew had had sexual relations with a young Indian woman, a *sannyasini* by another guru. She had confessed and been full of remorse, but he had admitted nothing. Master said to the swami that he was seeing dark clouds in his face and there surely must be something that created those clouds.

The young man was very proud and tried to minimize and gloss over the whole affair, as if it didn't really have any significance. But Master pointed out to him what serious karma he had created for himself because in some future life he would have to make the woman his rightful wife. Not only that, but he would have to give her a very happy life. Master also told him that he was very arrogant, very proud of his intellect, and that although he had made a conquest over a woman, he had failed as a *brahmachari*. He had proved he could not rely on the intellect that he thought was so superior.

The swami listened to all this with a stony face. Gurudev called his young assistant, Swami Christmas Tree, and asked him for a pair of *kartals*, which are an aid in drowning out the background noises of the mind. Giving these to the young swami he said, "In every woman Divine Mother is incarnated. Having worshipped her physical form and tasted the sweetness of it, you will now worship the Divine Mother in her spiritual form. You will stay in your room and chant her 108 names. I will have food sent to your kutir. You may go now." The swami *pranamed*, then bowed only very slightly and left.

Gurudev said, as if he knew already all the questions I was going to ask, "You must never serve any liquid, tea, coffee, milk, or anything like that, after 6 o'clock in the evening. You must get everybody out of bed by 5 o'clock in the morning and have them go to the bathroom immediately. The fullness of the bladder creates a sense that is easily changed by the mind to the desire for sexual activity."

He added, "Some of the yoga practices clog up the tubes in a man and a woman in due time, with regular practice, which reduces the sexual urges. The initiates have also known all the power of nature which wants to perpetuate itself. For everyone it takes several lifetimes before one can loosen the grip of nature. But always remember that the true union is not between two human bodies, however ecstatic such a union would be, but between your individual consciousness and Cosmic Consciousness."

I nodded my head as if I knew and understood exactly what he said, but I could see by Master's smile that he knew that my intuitive understanding had not yet grasped the meaning. I searched in my bag for the notebook he had given me. When I could not find it he handed me a piece of paper smilingly, and let me hang around to jot down these most important explanations. He continued, "Always remember only gods can walk the rainbow; always think of yourself as the eternal Radha. Never look back as you walk the rainbow. When you look back you fall down farther than anyone else could."

I was about to leave when Gurudev's voice held me back. "Are you practicing the mantras?" he asked me.

I answered in the affirmative but mentioned that I had great difficulty with the last one, while the first three of the four he had given me came rather easily.

He said that I must try. "You see, I want you to initiate people on my behalf. Each mantra represents a different aspect of the Lord. People need a mantra that suits their temperament and their character. Unless you acquire the power of the mantra the initiation is worthless."

I looked at Gurudev in horror and said, "This is a formidable task—acquiring the power of four mantras, especially with the fourth one seeming not to sit with me at all."

But Gurudev waved this off saying, "If God gives the work, He gives the tools. He gives the strength, He gives the courage."

As he went back to his work, I *pranamed* and left his kutir. As always, I went to the Ganges and my favorite rock. I sat there with a tremendous sense of loneliness. I felt a great sense of responsibility weighing on me. A formidable task! After some time a feeling of peace and serenity settled over me. I have no explanation of where it came from. For the first time, I did not seek Swami Chidananda, Swami Venkatesananda, or any of the other swamis who always had been very helpful.

I had been practicing mantras to help me understand the workings of the mind, for a mantra is an extremely useful tool to stop the merry-go-round, the mental conversations, the constant dialogues I was holding with myself. The regular use of a mantra was a tremendous strain on time, a demand on my patience, self-control in the ability to sit still. But the power of the mantra! To acquire the power of the mantra seemed to be an impossibility. And four of them! Maybe I am fooling myself trying to achieve a sense of peace through mantras. But maybe it is rather a matter of God's grace. Gurudev talks a lot about God's grace, and that goodwill and trying one's best can bring God's grace into action. Suddenly I had a new surge of energy, joyful energy! Gurudev told me that in a mantra I could also use the name of Jesus. He said that the objective is not to make Christians into Hindus. "You teach them only the practices—the way yoga is used by many religions. It is not itself a religion, but a scientific way of life."

12 February

*M*r. *Brown is a very different* type of visitor — a lawyer who recently arrived at the ashram from the United States. We walked to Gurudev's kutir from the office. Mr. Brown addressed Gurudev, "Swamiji, you have made a lady a swami and will have her do some work in the West. This will create great difficulties. While the Western woman's position cannot be compared with that of an Indian woman, nevertheless I do not know of any field in which women have leadership. Why don't you send one of your male swamis who would also impress the public much more?"

Gurudev stopped, looked at him, and said, "Yes, I know it will be more difficult for her, but women do not have the same temptations that men have. The worship of women everywhere is a man's downfall. Success in any undertaking of a spiritual nature is always with the Lord."

Mr. Brown did not say any more about this, but when Master had stopped speaking, he used this opportunity to say, "I came here," almost begging with his eyes, "for a particular purpose. I have read Eastern philosophy. I think I understand what yogis talk about, but so far it is all theory and perhaps because I am a lawyer I cannot believe that something like reincarnation exists. I have read in the books," the lawyer continued, "that yogis can, by a transmission of power, awaken the past for a follower with a simple touch. I want to assure you that it is not just curiosity that leads me to ask you to let me have such an experience. I have searched myself and I am pretty clear. If I could have such an experience I could accept all the other parts of the philosophy."

Master started walking very slowly, as did all of us. My mind was speculating about the same thing. Was it not unfair to demand faith in something unknown, never experienced?

Master came to a stop. He turned to the lawyer, facing him directly. "I cannot give you this experience, but I will not let you go empty-handed."

I wondered if Gurudev had tuned in to this man and so was convinced of his sincerity. I was very curious to know what he would give him. Now Master explained in great seriousness that Mr. Brown should begin on a Monday evening to write down everything he had experienced that day, put it in an envelope, seal it and put the date on it. Every day of the week he should do the same thing. On Sunday Mr. Brown was to sit down and write all that he could remember that had happened during the week. Following this he was to open all the envelopes, check his memory and see how his mind had changed and twisted some of the incidents. The next Monday he was to begin again, but this time he was to take stock after two weeks, then three weeks and so on. Master said it would take him about two years before he would recall past life incidents by that method. He also said to Mr. Brown, "The present condition of your central nervous system does not allow the experience of a past life right now. Having acquired an experience yourself, you will also be more inclined to accept it."

I found that answer strange and made up my mind that I would ask Gurudev more about it. My opportunity came sooner than I had hoped for because he called me into his kutir to give me some more work. I asked him right then and there. Can such power transmission be done? What has it to do with the central nervous system, or was he just keeping the man pacified?

Master laughed, "No, no, no. The man is a lawyer in this life for a reason. He was hanged innocently in a past life and he died with an earnest desire for justice, as a soul can do which has been treated unjustly. He also had to struggle unusually hard because of karma to become a lawyer."

With that, Master dismissed me and I thanked him once again for having satisfied my desire to know. However, the other part of my desire was not yet satisfied. I sought out the company of Mr. Brown almost immediately, before he could talk to anybody else, and invited him to come along for a walk. He very happily consented and I asked him how he felt about Gurudev's "recipe" for past lives or reincarnation experiences. He admitted he had only a vague idea, but he could certainly see there would be a tremendous strengthening of the mind and memory by such discipline.

Then I asked him rather diplomatically, "Why did you become a lawyer?"

He told me his life story. His father had died when he was a small boy, his mother had married again, his step-father had thrown him out at 14, telling him to make his own living. "I had to put myself through school by working weekends and nights, and many of my meals came by being invited by the parents of my school friends. I studied hard. I wanted to go to university. I wanted to become a lawyer."

That fitted perfectly well with what Gurudev had just told me. The determination that he brought into this life had its foundation in the intense desire at the time of death and I could see that reliving the experience of his execution would be too much for a man who had had such a hard time in this life. I could see that by the slow recall the emotions would gradually adjust to be able to handle the experience. We returned slowly to the ashram from our walk, each being absorbed in our own thoughts.

Mine were speculating on what may have triggered my present life and why I cannot recollect having been with Gurudev and worked with him before. I have learned by now also to make an attempt to step outside my mind and just watch it running in circles and even be amused by it. I decided I was now here, living on this earth, and because of that I had to live this life in such a way as not to repeat past mistakes. And I will rethink all my desires, so when I have to leave this earth, at the time of my death I will leave with the right desire on my mind. I don't want to get tangled up again. The price for every little pleasure that life has to offer is simply too high. Letting go, letting go of the pain—that is what Master always says. I must burn that into my mind. That would give me many blessings. At this moment I am happy to be a *sannyasini*.

13 *February*

It was about 2 o'clock in the morning when Swami Bliss knocked on my door and woke me, saying that the Master would like to see me. I was wondering what it could be that he would call me for in the middle of the night. When I came he offered me a place on the bench and said, "I want you to go back to the West to do some work for me. I don't want you to take a job. I want you to live by faith alone. People have to witness that God, Who created everything, can also take care of His creation. What will be the first thing you do when you go back?"

"I will take a course in English for proper grammar and pronunciation and then a course in public speaking for talking to audiences."

"None of this," Gurudev waved it aside, "then you talk from the mind. You must let God take over."

"But people will think I am a fool."

"All right then, be God's fool. When you go back, you must just await developments. Everything will fall into place. Always think of yourself as Radha. When you can do this you will have incredible power at your disposal."

Master handed me a fruit and I gave him my *pranam* and left. I could not sleep. When it was light enough in the early morning I went to the Ganges, still thinking about this order. I felt like crying, but I could not. For the first time I realized what those famous words meant, "The birds have a nest and the fox has a hole, but I have no place to lay my head." There are no family members I can ask for help. There are no friends who can understand my step into this type of life. There is nothing in the cultural tradition I come from that would support it. A lot of things I have known intellectually, but the actual experience is a very different matter. The reality of the homelessness and the loneliness of my path really overwhelms me.

14 *February*

Swami Chidananda had informed me

that it was necessary to have a formal initiation according to tradition and that the usual time is December or March. I tried to convince him to have it earlier, if it was possible that an exception could be made, because my visa would be terminated by March. I felt it was important that I should have the opportunity to stay at the ashram for a while afterwards, in case the formal initiation should affect me as the other one had. Fortunately he was able to arrange this.

The time is set in conjunction with sunset. I took a bath in the Ganges, put on a fresh sari — the white silk with the red and gold border that Gurudev liked best — and made my way to his kutir, with the garlands, fruits and flowers that the disciple is expected to bring. I was counting on Swami Venkatesananda's help because his kutir was so close to Gurudev's. Satchitanandaji received me. He knew what I came for and when we entered Master's veranda, I gave him my *pranam*. He smiled when Gurudev said, "Get me a big pair of scissors. Radha has a lot of hair." I was prepared to have my head shaved, but imagined that I would look very funny with hair cut off with scissors and was wondering when the barber next came to the ashram.

Swami Bliss set up everything needed, organized the details like fruit, flowers, milk, water, in proper relationship to each other, then told me what to do as the ceremony advanced. Finally Gurudev said, "Bend your head," took a bunch of hair from the back and I heard the sound of the hair being cut by the scissors. Then he handed it to me and told me to go down to the Ganges, and throw it into the river, take three sips of the water, reciting the mantra, and then come back. Everything was so new and strange. There wasn't much time to have my own thoughts and make any assessment. I just carried out the command and returned as quickly as possible. A few more mantras, more milk, more water poured over Master's feet, then came the moment when the orange clothes that were lying by his feet were handed to me and he invited me to change in his quarters.

I had never seen the inside except what was visible from the door. I was disappointed. There was not much to see. He had a huge bed of European style and there was a door to a small cabinet that seemed to be his private toilet. By noticing these things I considered myself so aware and clear-headed that I almost thought I was not responding properly. But I had no time to think about those things. Gurudev elaborated extensively on what it meant to be a *sannyasi*, about conduct, that I should not answer any questions about the past, nobody should even know my name, I should not let my own mind dwell on the past but have a steady gaze towards the Light. A few more *pranams* and he picked up one of the garlands I had brought to him and put it around my neck. With that I was dismissed. Young Satchitananda took it on himself to put Gurudev's quarters in order.

A few days later Chidananda handed

me a document confirming that my initiation was according to tradition, that I was now Swami Radhananda. He suggested that Gurudev's decision that I should be called Swami Sivananda Radha was right and I should leave it that way, but I needed to know that by tradition I would be Swami Radhananda. He also said that he had talked to Master and I would receive a document that would give express authorization of what I was supposed to do—deliver lectures, initiate others, start centers, etc. Chidananda at this point wanted to be really helpful and he said that there would be the official document for me and a copy sent to the Indian Embassy in Canada. He would also give me a shorter one that I could use for display. In America everything is displayed, he joked.

I thought it funny that a *sannyasa* initiation needed to have a document of authorization, but I supposed that someday it might be helpful, so I thanked him for his consideration.

Venkatesananda motioned me to leave the kutir and I followed him to his place. I asked him why Gurudev did not cut off all my hair. I had expected him to do so.

Very surprised, Swami Bliss said, "Really, what would people say if you went back to America with your head shaven?"

It seemed irrelevant and I said, "But I am still here. I want to know why Master did not do that. Was my initiation really a formal one?"

He assured me, "Of course. But because you did not make any fuss, because you were willing to renounce your hair, it was enough to take only a small amount to fulfill the ritual itself."

* * * * *

FAREWELL TO SRI SWAMI SIVANANDA RADHA
Swamiji's speech on 21.2.56

This is a glorious day, an auspicious day, a joyful day. We have amongst us a Canadian Yogi. We are offering our highest tributes and homage to her for her Divine virtues and practice of Yoga and her strongest desire to live in the Eternal and to disseminate the knowledge of Yoga-Vedanta in the West.

Her coming here from far off Canada to meet me is not an accidental chance. It is in the Grand Plan, the working of Prarabdha. We lived together and worked together in the field of spirituality in a past life, so we have met here in this birth. Sivananda Radha (Sivananda—Master's name; Radha—Eternal companion of Krishna) has come with intense desire, faith and devotion, to meet me and to learn something of Yoga—not to learn, she already knows Yoga, only the Samskaras (impressions), which are already engraved in her mind have to be brought back to the surface of consciousness. Her virtues are in abundance. Her adaptability is unique and unparalleled. She is amicable, moved by all people, showing her kindness and affection. She is a very earnest student, full of energy and tenacity of purpose. She went to Dehra Dun   a new science, our Bharata Natya, in a short space of time without knowing the language. Mr. Devasatyam taught only in Tamil, and she learned Tal, rhythm, the movements and the expressions, with the heart, most wonderful. It is very difficult for others to learn as much within a month.

Her devotion to the Guru is most unique and unparalleled. She worked day and night and gave a good deal of work for her music teacher, Swami Nada Brahmanandaji also—four hours daily. Nada Brahmanandaji is also a Swami of calm serenity. He never gets irritated when people bore him for four or five hours. He is ever ready to help the students in music and he has elevated and instructed hundreds of people here, and in Dehra Dun, Roorkee and various other places. He is a most kind musical teacher and professor who is an adept in the science of Thaan in music.

Yogic students feel that a Yogi can fly in the air, walk on the water and do other miracles. They think then only you know Yoga. It is a sad mistake. To be peaceful, to be calm, to radiate joy, to have an intense aspiration and devotion, to have a spirit of service—this is Yoga. This is not so easy. Flying in the air is not Yoga. Why become a bird after so many years of Sadhana (spiritual practice) and Pranayama (life force, breath)? Even Nirvakalpa Samadhi (heightened state of Divine ecstasy) is not necessary for us. You must have a willing heart to serve everybody, the spirit of service and a desire to possess all divine virtues. This is Yoga. Let us not try to become a bird and fly to Delhi. Five or six rupees is enough to go to Delhi.

To be good, to do good—this should be our ideal. Be ever willing to share what you have with others. You should have knowledge of scriptures, devotion to teacher, to saints, and to founders of religions. Why do you want to get yourself merged in the Absolute? Possess Divine qualities and move as a Divine Being. Freedom from hatred, malice, readiness to share with others — such things you should possess.   Merging in the Absolute is not necessary. Let us have a small veil of individuality, and serve here as Nityasiddhas (eternal perfect ones). You elevate thousands of people by your example. You remain as a Divine Being on this earth. So let us not aspire for powers only. Powers come by themselves, and we do not want them. Remain as a Divine Being. Possess all the Divine virtues that are enumerated in the Gita (spiritual scripture of India). Share what you have with others. This is Yoga.

So, Sivananda-Radha will do a great deal of work in America and Canada through her practice of Yoga, guiding groups of people, elevating them, giving them the message of the Rishis, sages and seers: "Satyam Vada" (speak the truth), "Darmam Chara" (lead a righteous life), "Worship mother as God, worship father as God, worship teacher as God, worship guest as God."

Swami Venkatesananda, Radha, and Swami Nadabrahmananda play Indian musical instruments on the banks of the Ganges.

Give, but give with modesty. Give with good will. Give with humility. That is the teaching that she will spread there. There is one eternal Atman (the Self), One Universal Consciousness dwells in the heart of all. Realize this through concentration, purification, aspiration, renunciation. So many 'tions are there. Therefore we must practice all these. Give, love, share. Control anger. Do not get irritated through misunderstanding. Understand everybody, their feelings. Bear insult. Bear injury. Then you yourself can fly in the air like a bird. After undergoing so much spiritual practice, do not aspire to become a bird.

If you develop one virtue, Satyam or truthfulness, all virtues will follow. You will become a magnet. Be ever intent on the welfare of all (Sarvabhootahiteratah). Even if a man is trying to take away your life with a dagger, be kind to him like Jesus. Love that man who tries to persecute you. These are the things you should practice, not only studying the Brahma Sutras and the Upanishads (spiritual scriptures of India): the Upanishads should come from your heart through purification, through service. Service is the highest thing on this earth. Service will make you Divine. Service is Divine Life. Service is eternal life in God. Service will give you Cosmic Consciousness. It is not easy. You will have to kill your egoism. You will have to pulverize your egoism, make it a powder like our Kahudavardhak (holy ashes). You have to make oil from your bones and burn it for six months. If you have humility all virtues will come by themselves. Sivananda-Radha has already got all these divine virtues. Do not become nervous. Be strong. Have a small beginning in the small room on the third floor in your house. Become a magnet. All will come, like bees to drink the honey. Gradually your work will spread throughout Canada and America. Those who want inner life are very few. All are thirsting to drink the honey, but they do not know where to drink that honey. They try to drink that honey from bank balance and helicopter. Maya (illusion) is very clever. Maya never allows anyone to taste the honey, to lead an inner life. Deluded by Maya, people say, "there is no transcendental realm."

There is nothing beyond the senses. Eat, drink and be merry. Have good tea and good coffee. You may remain here for two years, but only for those who have the grace of the Lord, the road is open. Many people leave the practice after five or six years, because there is no real aspiration. They have only some curiosity. They want to get psychic powers to become a Yogi and start an Ashram. Only for those people who sit in the Dattatraya Temple or on the bank of the Ganges and practice Japa (Yoga of repetition of the Divine Name) and concentration is the road open. You need not to go to Dattatraya Temple. What a beautiful scenery: Vyasa and other Rishis remained here. Their vibrations are in the Akasic (etheric) record. This is the best place in the world for meditation. Mussoorie (city in the Himalayas) may be tempting, but this is the best place for meditation. Let us become Yogis.

Swami Radha will do a lot of work there in Canada and America and change the people there. Let her not be diffident, but confident. Even three months practice on the Ganges bank is sufficient for an earnest student.

Be good, do good. This is the essence of the teachings of all the scriptures and of all the prophets of the world. So we all pray for her long life, peace, prosperity, Tushti (contentment), Pushti (nourishment) and all Divine Aiswaryas (Divine powers).

* * * * *

FAREWELL TO SRI SWAMI SIVANANDA RADHA
Swami Chidanandaji's Speech on 21.2.56

Revered Immortal Atman,

Today we are having a farewell function with a special and auspicious significance. There is a seeker from the West who, having come as a devotee, has stayed here for some months and is now going back, not as one returning home, but as one who has become a fellow in our own order, a Gurubhai or Gurugbshin, and

The author dancing on the Ashram temple steps.
Through prayer dance the body can be refined as a spiritual tool
to express devotion to the Most High.

now she belongs to Ananda Kutir, being one among the circle of the monastic disciples of Sri Gurudev. . .

. . .In these six months that she has been here I think amongst all the people who have come from outside India, very few people have endeared themselves so very universally to all people in Ananda Kutir as Mother Radhananda has done. She has entered into the heart of everyone, even people with whom she has no means of communication, people who do not understand a word of English. One instance in point: Mother Tara of Swargashram felt that Radha was her own sister. She said, "I cannot explain it, I cannot talk to her, but I felt as if I am meeting my own sister." This is what the school children also say. . . That is because she has identified herself with Ananda Kutir. She has never felt that she is someone from outside who is remaining here for some time. She felt this to be her home, and she is a true and earnest seeker. There have been people who have remained here for some days, weeks, months and have left with a feeling of dissatisfaction here, with a feeling that they have not fulfilled the purpose for which they have come. And they have also felt that, "no one has taken any particular interest in us. . .and we have been neglected, no one has approached us with overflowing spiritual knowledge." But why is it that she has not felt like that? Why is it that she has not had the feeling of being neglected? Because the intensity of her aspiration is real. . .this genuine aspiration has not made her sit quietly expecting others to come and offer their knowledge to her, saying, "Come along, I will teach you, I will train you." No. From the very day she came here she has been trying to contact each and every one. "What can this man teach me? What can that Swami give me?" She has been approaching everyone, approaching in a sweet way full of apologies.

She has been an aggressive aspirant, an aggressive seeker. The knowledge she has acquired in six months may take six years to digest and assimilate. Swamiji gives enough to an aspirant in a single day to keep him engaged for a whole life. I do not know all the things she has learned—music, Indian dance, singing, Yogasanas from Vishnudevananda, Vedanta from Krishnananda.

202 .

Farewell to Sri Swami Sivananda Radha. Gathering on the roof of an ashram building, Sivananda Ashram, Rishikesh, India, 1956.

She used to put so many intricate questions to me. . .and she has not spared anyone. She has always been busy. It is an example of how aspirants should be, not waiting for knowledge to come into our lap, but chasing knowledge that is trying to escape and grasping it. . .

And as a fellow disciple, what is Swami Radhananda to us? Swami Radhananda to my vision appears as an embodiment and personification of five or six very sublime spiritual qualities. She has simply overwhelmed me with one characteristic in particular. That is her faith. I say this because of the inner knowledge I have about the manner in which she has been tested. Her faith has been tried severely, and if it was anyone else but Mother Radha, I think they would have packed up and left long ago. But curiously and inexplicably, each test and severe trial that her faith had to undergo has only served to make it stronger and more firm. I feel this is so because her faith was deep-rooted. It was well grounded, and that faith itself is sufficient to take her to God Realization. During her six month's stay in Ananda Kutir, Mother Radhananda has won victory, and I am sure that the grace of Gurudev and the blessings of God will shower upon her the fruit of her victory. She has the Divine, true faith. To that I bow in humble reverence.

Her second great spiritual quality is devotion—Gurubhakti. And in that also she has overcome all obstacles that stand in the way of sustained devotion. If you have devotion to a personality for certain particular qualities and for love's sake, not because a person has got a pair of wings and can fly, not because of anything else but because of the person being himself, that is true devotion. Her Gurubhakti to the Guru is because He is a Guru. "I have accepted him as my Master; therefore, I will love Him with all my heart, with all my being." That is the love Christ had asked as the price for salvation, for the real descent of the grace of God, and it is such love that she is trying to develop. Devotion to the Master because he is the Master, and it is immaterial whether he is a supernatural being, whether he has got Yogic powers, or whether he will be able to solve all my problems.

And the next virtue is renunciation, renunciation of a superior order. She gave all her love at the feet of the Master, to the spiritual quest. Thus her attachment has been turned very effectively away from all those things she held very dear to her. It is not an easy job. Try to put yourself in her position and picture what coming over from that life to this life meant. . .to a Westerner, who came here with no conception of Sannyasa. For her to take such a step is something wonderful, and she has been able to overcome that hurdle and make an act of renunciation in the West in one of the busiest modern cities in Canada, giving up her job. They said, "We cannot give you leave. Either you do not take leave, or you resign the job." And she resigned her job. It shows the courage that is part of her character. She was a professional dancer. But she renounced that, an art to which she was attached.

And then humility—the humility of a seeker and a learner—this is another distinctive quality that you see in Mother Radhananda. She has learned at the feet of Gurudev the great secret that egoism, pride, the feeling of 'I-ness,' is the chief and greatest of all obstacles in the path of the seeker and aspirant, and this secret makes her a real seeker. The true Yoga is to overcome the mind, to overcome the ego. This is the real secret of Yoga and attainment of spiritual consciousness; when 'I' dies and mind is conquered, then alone Light Divine descends into the heart of man. Master Himself has become her heart. By observing him every moment, his word and action, she has been able to gather the real essence of Yoga and the real essence of Vedanta.

Let her carry on her Canadian work. Let her be always cheerful. Never for a moment let her think herself inadequate. All inadequacies will be overcome because Gurudev supports her. God dwells in all hearts. Let Gurudev work through our hands. Let Him remain in our hearts. Let His power animate us. That is the spirit in which we shall all work.

Therefore, we pray to the Lord and to the Lotus Feet of Gurudev that their grace and blessings may always be with her, wherever she goes across the seas, and may they enable her to do the great work of bringing thousands and thousands of eager and sincere seekers into the path of Divine Light that takes a being from darkness to Light, from death to immortality, that takes the being from this unreal world to the real world.

With these words of prayerful blessing, I conclude my offering in the form of this little talk at the feet of Swami Sivananda Radha.

1 March

My pilgrimage to India is over.

The plane takes me back to Canada. What an incredible half year it has been—all so foreign, yet so familiar. How critical I was in the first few weeks. Gurudev was very understanding. I wonder if understanding and forgiving are the same thing.

Swami Sivananda Radha. What is going to happen to Sylvia? How will I explain these two aspects of myself? I don't think that my letters to Elizabeth have made any sense to her. I hope she will be at the airport. It would be too difficult to return to the West and have everybody turn their backs on me. What will people think of my strange robe in this vibrant orange?

O my God! I will be arriving in about ten hours without any money! What will I do? How can I expect other people to look after me? How can I lecture or teach? And worst of all, how can I possibly start an ashram—and where will the people come from? I'm afraid my old friends will refuse to have anything to do with me. They have not even answered my letters from India.

Where will I go? My fear grows. It overrides everything I try to tell myself—that India had been a great experience, that I am most grateful for the spiritual experiences (but right now I cannot

206 ·

find any reassurance in them), that I am grateful for Swami Sivananda (but he seems to have stayed behind in the remote distance). I am going to need so much support and help in my new life, but where will that come from? Doubts are pouring into my head by the dozens. I cannot even decide if they are healthy or not. They are just there and I am very scared.

Maybe I should distract myself. All the magazines are taken. The stewardess comes through and offers drinks. I take one. At this moment nothing matters. I feel like crying. Suddenly there comes a feeling of great peace and stillness. It is as if Gurudev were sitting here beside me. I remember his words:

"I promise, I will be ever with you.
If you turn to your right — I will be on your right side.
If you turn to your left — I will be on your left.
But go ahead because I will be right in front of you.
We have lived and worked together in previous births.
Never forget that."

Swami Radha was born in Germany as Sylvia Hellman in 1911 and lived there until after World War II. Always of a very questioning nature, she soon realized that worldly success brought little of enduring value. The disruptive events in Germany through the war years only increased her desire to find a lasting and meaningful purpose in life.

After the war she immigrated to Canada and became a Canadian citizen. A visionary experience led her to her Guru, Swami Sivananda Saraswati of Rishikesh, India. At his ashram she received intense training in the philosophy and practices of yoga, and in 1956 she was initiated into the sacred order of sannyas as Swami Sivananda Radha.

At her Guru's request she returned to the West to open teaching centers for the study and practice of yoga. In Burnaby, British Columbia, she founded an ashram which later moved in 1963 to its present location in Kootenay Bay, B.C. In 1971 she founded the Association for the Development of Human Potential (A.D.H.P.), an American nonprofit organization dedicated to the study of mind and consciousness. To respond to the needs of increasing numbers of students in urban environments, Swami Radha opened several yoga teaching centers called Shambhala Houses where classes and courses are taught by teachers specifically trained at Yasodhara Ashram.

Swami Radha's major focus has been to interpret the ancient teachings of the East so that they can be understood and applied in the daily life of the Westerner. She has lectured all over North America at psychological institutes, universities, colleges, and spiritual centers and is the author of several classical books of yoga including *Kundalini Yoga for the West, Hatha Yoga: The Hidden Language, Mantras: Words of Power,* and *The Divine Light Invocation.* For more information on classes and courses write to the Program Secretary, Yasodhara Ashram, Box 9, Kootenay Bay, B.C. V0B 1X0, Canada.